Management Skills Series
Total Quality Management

Total Quality Management

A Total Quality Approach

GORDON F. GATISS

CASSELL

IN ASSOCIATION WITH THE INSTITUTE FOR SUPERVISION AND MANAGEMENT

Cassell
Wellington House, 125 Strand, London WC2R 0BB
215 Park Avenue South, New York, NY 10003

British Library Cataloguing-in-Publication Data
A catalogue record for this book is available from the British Library.

ISBN 0-304-33795-1 (paperback)

Typeset by Kenneth Burnley at Irby, Wirral, Cheshire.
Printed and bound in Great Britain by Redwood Books, Trowbridge, Wiltshire.

Contents

TOTAL QUALITY MANAGEMENT:
A Total Quality Approach
by Gordon F. Gatiss

CUSTOMER FEEDBACK QUESTIONNAIRE

As a reader of this book your opinions are valued. To help me improve the quality of this product, would you take the time to complete the following questionnaire and return it to the address below.

Thank you.
Gordon F. Gatiss

Please print your name and address:

Post code:

Question 1
Was the subject explained in a way that was:

	Very well		Good		Not very well
a. easy to understand?	5	4	3	2	1
b. clear and concise?	5	4	3	2	1
c. relevant and meaningful?	5	4	3	2	1

Question 2
Did you find the book:

	Very well		Good		Not very well
a. enjoyable?	5	4	3	2	1
b. a learning experience?	5	4	3	2	1

Question 3
If you could change one thing in the book, what would it be?

If you wish to make further comments then please use a separate sheet.

Address to send all correspondence:
Cassell PLC, Professional Sector, Wellington House, 125 Strand, London WC2R 0BB.

Foreword

In today's highly competitive market place, being good enough is no longer good enough.

Customers' expectations are rising all the time and the successful businesses will always be those which remain passionate about continuously improving what they do. It was not long ago that a car with a three-speed fan heater was an optional extra, offered by few manufacturers. Through listening to what customers want and designing those features into cars, the successful manufacturers survive and prosper because customers are getting what they want.

Today air conditioning, compact disc players and many other 'gadgets' are becoming accepted as standard items and not optional extras. The pace of technological development is fantastic! There is more technology in the modern motor car than in the lunar buggy that landed on the moon in the 1960s. One desktop personal computer has more processing power than existed in the whole world prior to 1950.

Technology, as applied to business processes, is not enough: people add the value and make the difference. Highly trained, motivated people who are focused on providing excellent service to their customers are an essential ingredient in today's business environment.

A 'total quality approach' is about listening to customers, identifying what they want and striving to meet their requirements: *getting it right first and every time*. Obsession with quality leads to a culture of customer first, last and always.

The concept of a total quality approach is not new: its origins can be traced back over seventy years. Mass production focused on quantity, with superficial attention to quality – for example, things were made to specification. Over the years the focus has changed due to increasing competitive pressures and customers who are no longer willing to accept mediocre mass-produced goods. They now require a guaranteed level of quality consistently.

This book is designed to educate those first-line managers who are starting on the journey to Excellence. Each chapter concludes with an opportunity to reinforce the key learning points and prepare the reader for the next stage in the process. Tools and techniques help the reader to put the learning into practice.

Do not read the book just in case you might apply the concepts – *do read* the book and make a difference in your organization: today, tomorrow and for ever.

Eric Logan
Director of Quality
Royal Mail North Wales and North West

Acknowledgements

The author wishes to record his grateful thanks to the following people for their time and contributions in helping to write this book: Eric Logan; Tony Mottram; Bill Harris-Heffer; Bob Thomas; David K. Topping; Nigel H. Wilkinson; Penny Francis; and Roger Bradshaw.

True quality is always a team effort.

Introduction

AIMS AND OBJECTIVES OF THIS BOOK

- To explain in a simple and straightforward manner the basic concepts of a total quality approach to working in today's demanding and challenging environment.

- To show the benefits of using a disciplined approach to problem-solving.

- To examine the benefits of using the primary quality tools and techniques to analyze, measure and control events.

- To encourage and excite the reader to become interested in learning more about how to reach his full potential and improve his value and worth in the job market.

Why should you read this book – what is in it for you?

You do not need to read this book unless you can answer 'Yes' to one or more of the following questions:

- Are you looking to improve?
- Are you looking to do a better job?
- Are you looking for ways to improve your business results?
- Are you looking for ways to improve your leadership?
- Are you looking for ways to motivate yourself and others?
- Are you seeking greater satisfaction from your work?
- Do you want knowledge and skills which really work?

When asked why Royal Mail felt it necessary to embrace a total quality approach to their business, Eric Logan the Director of Quality for North West and North Wales said: 'It is simple: *Survival is not compulsory.*'

Why another book on total quality?

Any library with a well-stocked Management section will contain countless books dealing with total quality. Some of the publications are excellent, and others are less so – generally because many of the authors offer prescriptive, formulated recipes for introducing and implementing total quality – and are written to impress and persuade the 'management' of an organization of the many benefits involved. They are often not read from cover to cover, but used as guides, with topics being browsed and skimmed.

This book has been written for the front-line worker, the person who actually does something in terms of performing an added-value function within an organization. It will be particularly useful to all front-line supervisors, support staff, those people involved in education and training, as well as the student and new employee who want to increase their value in the job market.

Part One distils and summarizes work by four influential writers on quality to build a foundation for the reader, showing where some of the ideas and concepts have come from. The narrative then proceeds to show how you can gradually learn to adopt a quality approach to work. Part Two introduces and explains a unique problem-solving discipline and takes the reader through ten effective and powerful practical quality tools and techniques for identifying, controlling and measuring. Part Three concludes with an holistic view of quality through the use of short, relevant case studies.

The book is structured into small learning steps, each one building on the last, with many opportunities throughout the work to reflect and grasp the concepts. For convenience, masculine pronouns are used throughout the book without any sexist intentions.

You cannot fail to gain some practical knowledge from reading this book. How effective that knowledge is, depends upon your desire for success. Success means doing the best you can with what you have. Success is a personal standard, reaching for the highest that is in you – becoming all that you can be.

I challenge every reader to take a quality approach and dare you to be your best.

GORDON F. GATISS
April 1996

Part One

A total quality approach should empower everyone to be
co-managers of their education.

The search for knowledge and improvement
should be something sought after
rather than something to be done.

The system must offer the chance to fail,
and then to learn from failure in order to improve.

CHAPTER 1

Background to a Total Quality Approach

AIMS AND OBJECTIVES OF THIS CHAPTER

- To introduce some influential writers on the subject of a total quality approach.
- To discuss what a total quality approach is.
- To encourage the reader to read Chapter 2.

This chapter summarizes some of the primary messages of four writers who have significantly influenced the author. The summaries are based on the following ideology:

- It is important to know where we have come from.
- It is essential to know where we are now.
- It is critical to know where we are going, why we are going and how we intend to make the journey.

INFLUENTIAL WRITERS AND CHAMPIONS OF QUALITY

1.1 Dr W. E. Deming

Dr W. Edwards Deming was born in 1900 and is regarded by the Japanese as the main architect for introducing Total Quality (TQ) principles into Japan after the Second World War. He graduated in electrical engineering from the University of Wyoming, and he gained a Ph.D. in mathematical physics from Yale. While working at The Western Electric Hawthorn plant in Chicago he discovered the work of Walter Shewart, the pioneer of controlled and uncontrolled variables and the statistical control of processes. Later he became a statistician for the US government. After the Second World War he was invited to go to Japan by General MacArthur in order to advise on the Japanese census. Deming's work led him to investigate quality control. The principle of Deming's philosophy is that quality is about people, not products.

Deming suggested a quality concept for designing a product. He defined the Product Development Cycle:

1. Design the product.
2. Make it.
3. Try to sell it.
4. Do consumer research and test the product's uses.
5. Redesign – start the cycle all over again.

Dr Deming stressed that management needed to understand the nature of variation and how to interpret statistical data. He stated that quality companies should direct their efforts towards:

- Innovation of products.
- Innovation of processes.
- Improvements of existing products.
- Improvement of existing processes.

The relevance of quality can be put into context by the following diagram showing the chain reaction of using a quality approach.

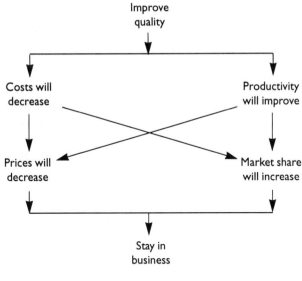

Figure 1.1

Dr Deming promoted the importance of leadership and he expressed the attributes of a leader as someone who:

- coaches – not judges;
- strives to understand variation and its causes;
- strives to remove obstacles from within the organization;
- responds to all customer forces;
- adopts consistency of purpose;
- places an emphasis on improving processes;
- recognizes that people are not 'assets'; they are 'jewels';
- strives to recognize those who need help and then gives help;
- creates an atmosphere of trust;
- knows the work he supervises;
- does not place an over-reliance on figures;
- encourages education and continuous improvement of each person.

He believed that 85 per cent of production faults were the responsibility of management, not the workers, and went on to formulate a fourteen-point management philosophy.

Deming's fourteen-point management philosophy

1. Create constancy of purpose for continual improvement of products and services.
2. Adopt a commitment to seek continual improvements.
3. Switch from defect detection to defect prevention.
4. In dealing with suppliers one should end the practice of awarding business on price. Move towards quality of product, reliability of delivery and willingness to co-operate and improve. Build partnerships.
5. Improvement is not confined to products and their direct processes but to all supporting services and activities.
6. Train in a modern way.
7. Supervision should change from chasing, to coaching and support.
8. Drive out fear and encourage two-way communication.
9. Remove barriers between departments.
10. Do not have unrealistic targets.
11. Eliminate quotas and numerical targets.
12. Remove barriers that prevent employees having pride in the work that they perform.
13. Encourage education and self-improvement for everyone.
14. Publish top management's permanent commitment to continuous improvement of quality and productivity.

**Create constancy of purpose
through encouraged training and education,
driving out fear.**

1.2 Peter Drucker

Peter Drucker was born in Vienna in 1909. He first came to Britain in the late 1920s and found a job as an apprentice clerk in a Bradford wool-exporting firm. Between 1933 and 1936 he worked as an economist in a London merchant bank. He emigrated to the United States in 1937, writing his first book in 1939 after which he took a job as a consultant with General Motors in 1942. Drucker's five basic principles of management are:

1. Setting objectives.
2. Organizing.
3. Motivating and communicating.
4. Establishing measures of performance.
5. Developing people.

Drucker believed that the ultimate key to success was threefold and involved knowing: what business you are in; what competences you have; how to keep focused on your goals.

He perceived that businesses survived or failed based on the bottom line, and that goals and objectives should be clearly defined. He always emphasized the importance of effective management and participation of employees by making the best use of all available human resources.

His writings indicate his belief that there are few differences between managing a business, a diocese, a hospital, a university, a research lab, or a government agency. He stresses that management should not deal with power but with responsibility. He writes 'The purpose of a business lies outside itself – that is in creating and satisfying a customer. The decision process is central, and structure has to follow strategy and management has to be management by objectives and self control.'

He was probably the first business writer to see the link between the bottom line and the purpose of satisfying the customer.

Modern quality management does not over-emphasise objectives as the most important aspect of management. Drucker's work on communication and performance controls helped develop the ideas and concepts of today's business practices.

**Know what you are, what you can do,
and keep focused on improvement.**

1.3 Charles B. Handy

Charles Handy was born in 1932 in Kildare, Ireland. After graduating from Oriel College, Oxford he worked for Shell International in Malaysia and then as an economist in London before joining MIT's Sloan School of Management.

Handy warns that in the business organization, as in many other areas of life, the status quo will no longer be the best way forward. Organizations that do not seek continuous improvement will lose market share and eventually be taken over or die. He suggests that this same analogy should be applied to people: if individuals do not continuously seek improvements in their working practices and behaviours or do not seek to add value to their existing skills over their lifetime, then they will not fit into the new working environment.

He has introduced the concept of a shift away from lifetime employment in a single company to portfolio work that will be less secure but more fulfilling. People will contract out their labour and may have more than one job. Increasingly he has shown concern with how companies manage their goals beyond the pursuit of profit. He fears that the Western model of company-as-property will prevail over the Eastern model of company-as-community.

In his works he emphasises the motivational aspects of participation, delegation and empowerment. He writes about quality attitudes and the need to involve all employees in finding solutions to the problems of waste within the organization. He introduces the concepts of being customer-orientated where everyone takes responsibility and there is a mature cultural philosophy throughout the business. He suggests aspects that we all need to consider are the issues of change created through:

- the communications and technology revolution;
- the fact that wages are a cost – fees are paid to add value;
- the fact that machines need servicing, maintenance and become inflexible and obsolete – tools can adapt and be modified and extend the capabilities of the individual;
- the economics of quality – the need to get it right first time, every time, consistently, adding value to the product by reducing or eliminating waste.

In *Understanding Organisations* Handy writes, 'Organizations which can allow old ways to die and new ways to grow will survive and have the chance to prosper. The acceptance of death as the prelude of life is a recipe for the survival of nature, society and the human race. It also applies to organizations.'

The status quo will no longer be the best way forward.

1.4 Tom J. Peters

Tom Peters was born in 1942. He worked in the Pentagon where he became fascinated by complex organizations. He then took a master's degree in civil engineering at Cornell University before serving in Vietnam. He went on to take an MBA at Stanford. He joined the consultancy group McKinsey in 1974, where he met Robert H. Waterman Jr.

Peters and Waterman had their greatest success with the publication *In Search of Excellence*. They analyzed forty-three companies and found that there were eight basic characteristics shared by all of them:

1. A bias for action – getting on with it.
2. Close to the customer – learning from the people they serve.
3. Autonomy and entrepreneurship – fostering innovation.
4. Productivity through people – treating the rank and file as a source of quality.
5. Hands-on, value-driven, committed management.
6. Stick to the knitting – stay with the business you know.
7. Keep things simple with a lean staff.
8. Empower your people, but have good measures and controls in place.

Five years after the book's publication two-thirds of the companies mentioned hit trouble in varying degrees. Peters and Waterman concluded from this that nothing in today's business environment stays the same for long. They concluded that excellent firms believed only in constant improvement and constant change.

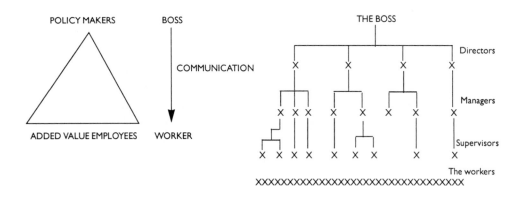

Figure 1.2

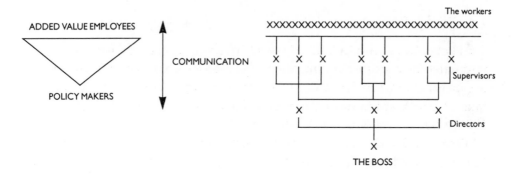

Figure 1.3

Peters has evolved a concept that organizations should move from a hierarchical management pyramid (Figure 1.2) to a horizontal, fast, cross-functional co-operative organization (Figure 1.3):

Peters evolved some guidelines to which people at every level should adhere:

- Actively create a quality revolution.
- Put the customer first in everything you do.
- Listen actively to all stakeholders.
- Invest in people, training, education and recruitment.
- Openly reward, recognize and support productivity innovation.
- Openly support failures where people have tried to improve.
- Involve everyone in everything at all times.
- Set up simple and understandable measures.
- Fight against bureaucracy and inflexibility.
- Look through a different mirror: step outside the company and look at it from a different perspective.
- Team-work and trust: develop strong interpersonal and team skills.
- Work on attitudes and attention to detail: get things done.
- Be consistent and strive for improvements in all areas.

Get close to the customer and stick to the knitting.
Keep things simple with a lean staff.
Be proactive, listen and invest in people
through training and education.

1.5   Summary of what a total quality approach is

A total quality approach (TQA) is all about improving in a structured way. It is clear from the many writers on the subject that total quality is involved with *change*. Each writer focuses on different elements that he feels are necessary. They all agree, however, that to survive and compete it is necessary for people and organizations to reassess their roles continually and strive to improve on an ongoing basis.

A total quality approach requires perpetual improvement.

A total quality approach therefore deals with two distinctive areas:

- The individual person: attitude.
- The organization: process.

The first lesson of a total quality approach is to recognize that as people, each of us produces a product. That product is usually the time and skill we bring to a job. We can refer to it as *our personal value*. It is this personal value, this ability to do something – to contribute and add value to an organization – that results in a reward called payment, salary or wages. Your ability to deliver total quality in everything you do depends upon your attitude.

All organizations make or produce something of value: this is often called a *product*. This product could be an actual tangible item like a loaf of bread or a computer; or it may be an invisible product referred to as a *service*, examples of which include a taxi service, a hospital, or perhaps providing insurance or personal advice and help as a charity, like the Citizens' Advice Bureau. The process involved in delivering the organization's product can only be total quality if all waste and inefficiencies have been eliminated.

Our attitude is not determined by circumstances, but by how we respond to circumstances. Our mindset determines our actions in given situations: we can respond positively or negatively. It is how we react to events, not the events themselves, which determines our attitude.

Changing attitudes and developing skills to deliver quality can be taught; however, these skills are only of quality if the knowledge gained from the training and education in the use of such skills can be applied and effectively used.

A total quality approach is a philosophy,
which continuously seeks to eliminate waste,
and endeavours to promote a commitment
to improve the quality in life, through working together.

What each of us does every day is our individual **PRODUCT**:
make that product one of **QUALITY**

TEST YOUR UNDERSTANDING

The purpose of the following questions is to reinforce the issues raised in Chapter 1 and to make them relevant to each reader. Where possible discuss your answers with a colleague or better still your departmental manager.

Question 1
Use the organization you work in or an organization with which you are familiar.

Using Deming's fourteen-point management philosophy, identify how many of the points raised are successfully employed in your chosen organization.

Question 2
A total quality approach deals with two distinct areas, that of people and process.
a) Look at yourself and list the competences and skills you possess as an individual.
b) Look at the organization in which you work, or an organization with which you are familiar, and list the processes within it which you feel are particularly good.

Question 3
Use the organization you work in or an organization with which you are familiar.

Peters and Waterman in their book *In Search of Excellence* identified eight basic characteristics that were shared by the organizations analyzed. How many of these characteristics can you identify in your chosen organization?

CHAPTER 2

Why Do Organizations Need a Total Quality Approach?

AIMS AND OBJECTIVES OF THIS CHAPTER

- To provide the reader with an understanding of the main objective of any organization.

- To provide an understanding of the differences between the external customer and the internal customer.

- To introduce the necessity for cost control.

- To introduce a structured methodology for planning improvements.

- To encourage the reader to read Chapter 3.

2.1 What is the main objective of any organization?

To answer the question of why organizations need a total quality approach to business, we should first determine what the main objective of an organization is.

There are two main types of business organization:

1. Commercial organization.
2. Not for profit organization (NFP).

Both these types of organization need to ensure that the money coming in exceeds the money going out. In the case of the commercial organization this is termed *profit*. In the case of the NFP organization this is termed *surplus*.

In reality there is no difference between profit and surplus, except the emotive use of the word 'profit' when referred to in relation to an NFP like a hospital or caring institution. Nevertheless if an NFP only succeeded in balancing its annual income and outgoings, then every year it would need to get more income just to stand still.

It is reasonable to expect small increases in running costs every year, such as improved salaries for the staff, increased fuel bills, transportation costs, stationery costs. Income would need to be made available to replace worn-out equipment and to invest in new technologies.

Even NFP organizations must plan for surplus money, otherwise they would need to make cuts every year.

It is therefore possible to say that

**the main objective of any organization is
to make a financial surplus.**

To achieve this main objective, any organization must fulfil three main criteria:

1. Satisfy customers.
2. Control costs.
3. Plan for improvements and growth.

The saleable element generated by the organization, whether it be a physical commodity or a service, is called *the product*.

The products provided by an organization are the means by which the main objective is achieved.

2.2 Satisfy customers – what is a customer?

The *Oxford English Dictionary* defines a customer as: 'One who buys, especially regularly, from one seller.' Unfortunately this definition has shortcomings when applied to a customer in a quality approach environment.

Questions:
- When a person buys a postage stamp and sends a letter, who is the customer: the person who bought the stamp or the person who receives the letter?
- When a parent buys a teddy bear for their son or daughter, who is the customer: the person who paid for the teddy bear or the person who will use and play with the teddy bear?
- Are the people who seek help from the Citizens' Advice Bureau or the Samaritans customers? If not, who is?

The person who buys a stamp from a post office is an external customer to the post office business. That person is a paying user of the stamp: the stamp provides a service that delivers the letter to the recipient. The recipient is the final customer even though he did not pay for the stamp, therefore he is, in reality, the user-only customer.

When a parent buys a toy for a child, the parent is the paying non-user customer: the child is the user-only customer.

When a person seeks advice from the Citizens' Advice Bureau or Samaritans, he is a user-only customer, better known as a *client* or *patient*. The paying customers are usually paying non-user customers, better known as *donors* or *subscribers* (this can be the government, local authorities or the general public).

	Paying user	Paying non-user	Client or patient (user only)	Subscriber donor
PRODUCT				
SERVICE				

Figure 1.3: External customer matrix

There is a difference between the parent who buys a toy for a child, and the paying non-user customer subscribing or donating to the Samaritans. The difference is that the subscriber has expectations of performance that will influence his continued subscription or donation to the organization in question.

All the types of customer referred to in all the above instances are called *the external customer.*

For any organization to supply a product to a customer (a customer being a paying user, a paying non-user, a user only or a client or patient), a commercial transaction must take place somewhere, otherwise the organization cannot exist. These commercial transactions must be managed and must produce positive results; this means they must improve the value of the product or service whilst lowering costs. Put another way, it means ensuring costs do not exceed income.

It is important to know what types of customers influence your business, and in what way they contribute to your organization. Are they user-only or are they paying customers? Different types of customer will have different expectations of the organization.

Some organizations have many different external customers and some have what can only be termed as a 'special customer'. This 'special customer' is usually over and above the commercial customer – it is the environment and/or society. These organizations might well be involved in one of the following areas: pharmaceuticals; chemicals; agriculture; teaching; power; water.

I have been quite specific in the last few pages, dealing with external customers. The term 'external' implies that there is another sort of customer: an *internal customer.* Internal customer is the term used to describe the relationships inside the organization, between different functions, departments and people. The understanding of the importance of this internal relationship is crucial to the successful implemention of a total quality approach.

To make the concept clear it may be better if we use the longer term: *Internal customer–internal supplier relationship.*

We all have internal customers, people who we deal with every day in our working environment, who work for the same organization. They may work in the same department or another department, they may even work in a different division of the organization. The critical thing is that at some time in your working role you have to pass or receive information, instructions, paperwork or some other work-related element to or from these people.

In Figure 2.2, Person A is passing a report to his boss who is Person B. Person A is the internal supplier; Person B is the internal customer. If Person B was passing instructions to Person A that were work-related, then Person A would be the internal customer.

Figure 2.2

Think of yourself as a business that delivers a product called 'my job'; then think of your job as a business, delivering a quality product.

In Figure 2.3, the teacher is supplying knowledge to the students, therefore the students are the internal customers. When the teacher sets a task for completion by the students, then the students become the internal suppliers and the teacher becomes the internal customer. The external customer in this relationship is the eventual employer(s) of the students, *and* society.

**All customers have the responsibility to
help suppliers deliver quality.**

Figure 2.3

When you give something to someone that enables them to do their job, you are acting as an *internal supplier*. When you require something from someone to do your job, then you are the *internal customer*.

Consider this internal interaction between people as a *product*: an internal product that is needed for the well-being of the organization, which in turn implies that it has implications for the external customer.

If the organization is operating to its main objective of making a financial surplus, and it is trying to do this by satisfying customers, then it follows that any interaction internally will have implications for the external customer.

Not only does the quality of the internal relationships have an impact on the external customer, it also follows that the organization's success with external customers has an impact on the financial surplus of the organization.

Internal customer relationships can be improved by means of involvement and reward, as the following passage suggests:[1]

> A total quality initiative should aim to maximize the involvement of all employees in the achievement of objectives, by giving them a say in how their job can be done more effectively. Thus it increases job satisfaction. Some organizations recognize significant contributions to quality improvements by means of recognition awards, usually tokens (medallions or certificates), but sometimes also financial rewards. Awards allow management to indicate to all employees that it recognizes the achievements of individuals and treats quality improvement seriously. Recognizing individual contributions to the quality improvement process reinforces the message that management is committed to quality and achieves long-term motivation of the workforce.

**Therefore the internal customer relationship within an organization
has direct implications on the financial surplus
of that organization.**

This strong correlation between internal co-operation and external customer satisfaction is particularly emphasised by R. J. Howe, D. Gaeddart and M. A. Howe in *Quality on Trial*.[2] They state that when the relationship between internal customers and internal suppliers is less than satisfactory, then the external customer suffers.

Some employees have difficulty in getting their colleagues to meet their needs. Some employees may have to work extra hours to cover for incompetent colleagues. This means that the organization is not focused on meeting the requirements and expectations of the ultimate customer.

If external customers are not satisfied, then financial surplus will fall. The rationale for a total quality approach is not customer satisfaction, it is not even customer delight, but *profit* or increased financial surplus.

2.3 Control costs

In any organization it is necessary to identify negative costs – those costs which are wasted. These are as follows:

Overproduction:	Providing more than is actually needed at the time.
Waiting:	Elements of time spent adding no value to the business.
Movement:	Moving a product, service, data, information or people without adding value to the business.
Unnecessary inventory:	Spending money on goods, service, travel, information, or people without adding value to the organization.
Unnecessary actions:	Doing things that are not adding value to the business.
Defects:	Erroneous actions taken in the business.

Peters and Waterman, as well as Handy, identify that many organizations have negative costs of between 35 per cent to 45 per cent of total operating costs. It is the reduction and elimination of these costs that enables an organization to become more competitive. The total quality approach to running an organization focuses on identification and reduction of waste and inefficiencies.

Reducing negative costs can significantly increase profits, as Figure 2.4 shows.

The elimination of negative costs improves the bottom line of an organization on a long-term, ongoing basis, more effectively than reducing operating costs.

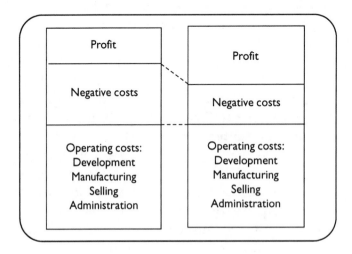

Figure 2.4

2.4 Plan for improvements and growth

A total quality approach emphasises participation, involvement and owner-ship of all the stakeholders in the organization. A stakeholder is someone who has an active involvement with the organization, as opposed to a pas-sive interest in the organization.

There can be many stakeholders in an organization, such as: employees; managers; shareholders; suppliers; all types of customer; governments; environment; and society.

A total quality approach to planning involves using a structured process like PANDA.

Prepare.
Act.
Navigate.
Do.
Assess.

Prepare: prepare a definition of the problem and a means of establishing the root cause.

Act: define positive action(s) that will measure criteria and confirm root cause, generating solutions.

Navigate: establish a planned route that will define objectives and deter-mine responsibilities for action.

Do: implement positive actions with measurable results.

Assess: actively assess the positive actions and establish the solution(s) as the new standard.

Using the PANDA approach to problem-solving involves the use of some quality tools such as:

- Team affinity brainstorming.
- Fishbone diagram.
- Pareto analysis.
- Bar charts/histograms.
- Force field analysis.
- Steady state control chart.

These tools and techniques will be discussed and explained to the reader later in the book.

2.5 Summary of why organizations need a total quality approach

We have established that organizations need a total quality approach to business to improve the financial surplus and bottom line of the company. A total quality approach enables this to be achieved by satisfying customers, controlling costs and planning for improvements and growth.

The rationale for a total quality approach
- *Financial surplus* is closely related to:
- *Customer retention.* It costs more to attract a new customer than it does to sell to an existing customer. Retaining 5 per cent more of existing customers could mean a 25 per cent to 100 per cent increase in profits: and the cost of attracting new customers could be fifteen times more than retaining an existing customer. Customer retention is closely related to:
- *Customer satisfaction* as perceived by the customer: this is usually a comparison of lifetime costs of the product. This is closely related to:
- *Customer support* which is likely to be high in organizations characterized by:
- *Employee retention* which is associated with careful selection of staff, effective training, empowerment and recognition and reward systems relating to performance. Employee retention stems from:
- *Employee satisfaction* which is high when:
- *Internal customer and supplier relationships* are effective.

TEST YOUR UNDERSTANDING

The purpose of the following questions is to reinforce the issues raised in Chapter 2 and to make them relevant to each reader. Where possible discuss your answers with a colleague or better still your department manager.

Question 1
Using the organization you work in or an organization with which you are familiar:
a) Identify the types of external customers.
b) Are all the different types of customer treated the same?

Question 2
a) List the internal customers who you have to relate to every week.
b) What *product* do you deliver to your internal customers?
c) Identify who your internal suppliers are, and what *product* they deliver to you.

Question 3
Using the organization you work in, or an organization with which you are familiar:
a) Make a list of all the negative costs categories you can identify in your own department.
b) Make a list of all the negative costs categories you can identify in the organization.

Question 4
Using the lists generated from Question 3, can you identify ways of putting a value on the negative costs identified?

Question 5
Without referring back to the relevant section, can you write down what the quality structured process PANDA stands for?

Notes to Chapter 2
1. *Productivity Management in Hospitality and Tourism,* edited by Nick Johns. London: Cassell, 1996; pp. 24–5.
2. *Quality on Trial,* R. J. Howe, D. Gaeddart and M. A. Howe.

CHAPTER 3

What Are Customer Requirements?

AIMS AND OBJECTIVES OF THIS CHAPTER

- **To explain who determines customer requirements.**
- **To identify factors affecting customer decisions to deal with an organization.**
- **To provide insight into customer satisfaction.**
- **To identify benefits sought by customers.**
- **To encourage the reader to read Chapter 4.**

3.1 Who determines external customer requirements?

In Chapter 2, I introduced the concept of external customers. One of the difficulties any organization has is determining precisely the true external customer requirements.

Many years ago it was acceptable to offer the customer what the organization thought the customer wanted. Competition was not as strong as it is today, and the customer was prepared to tolerate poor-quality products. Price was the discriminator in respect to quality and customers chose freely between a cheap alternative or the expensive original.

In the 1950s and 1960s most television sets were rented. There was a strong United Kingdom manufacturing industry that supplied the domestic market. Many outlets selling televisions established service and repair functions to cater for the growing market, as the television became a standard household requirement and no longer a luxury. It was said that outlets selling television sets made more money from their service and repair operations than they did from selling the original equipment.

In the early to mid-1970s the Japanese exported television sets that were different. These television sets were the same price as the domestic market set, but they did not break down as often: they were more reliable. The market was transformed within a very short space of time. Customers demanded the Japanese sets, and instead of renting they bought them.

Two major things happened:

- The service and repair functions had less and less work to do and over a few years many closed down which resulted in people losing their jobs.
- The United Kingdom television manufacturing industry reduced its prices: the Japanese did not respond, they simply maintained the quality of their product. The domestic manufacturers could not compete with the quality and reliability of the Japanese sets. Customers chose quality before price, with the result that the UK television industry collapsed.

The moral of the story is:

**Customer service is efficient
if it means putting right things which have gone wrong.**

**Customer service is effective
if the product is right first time and stays right.**

The Japanese had changed the rules – to compete in the market you had to change from being an efficient organization to being an effective organization.

Competing solely on price is based on the assumption that cost is the dominant factor in purchasing decisions. Experience has proved that this is not to be the case. Limited research carried out while working in the consumer and electronic industries has indicated that the factors affecting customer decisions to buy are in order of priority:

1. Product availability.
2. Product reliability.
3. Prompt attention to queries.
4. Manners and courtesy of organization's representatives.
5. Delivery time.
6. Price.
7. Brand name.
8. Accuracy of paperwork.
9. Product range.
10. Advertising.

Obviously there are exceptions, and only one thing is reasonably certain: that everything can and does change. If all other factors are equal then price may be the crucial discriminator that secures the business.

**It is better to out-think your competition
than to try to out-spend them.**

The external customer's requirement is only met when it is perceived to have been met by the external customer. Just doing what the external customer has asked for does not necessarily mean the external customer will be satisfied.

3.2   Who determines internal customer requirements?

The answer to this question is somewhat determined by the nature of the role played in the organization. However, the internal customer is the one who should determine his requirements (in the same way as the external customer). The true test is that the internal customer requirement should always be adding value to the organization. This internal added value should also add value to the external customers' requirements or the finished product, otherwise the process is a negative cost.

If the internal customer is asking you to provide a *product* (information, data, material or some other service) that is not adding value to the external customers' requirements, then the matter should be discussed urgently with the internal customer and the waste should be cut out.

The internal customer's requirement is only met when it is perceived to have been met by the internal customer. Just doing what the internal customer has asked for does not necessarily mean the internal customer will be satisfied.

3.3 Internal and external customer satisfaction

My own personal research has indicated customer sources of complaints in order of importance as:

1. Job not done right.
2. Too slow.
3. Too expensive.
4. Indifferent personnel attitude.
5. Unqualified personnel.
6. Lack of respect/courtesy.

This information is important in that it shows that competitive advantage can come from technical competency rather than courtesy of staff. As Tom Peters stated, 'Courtesy does not make up for junk.' A total quality approach is not solely about being nice to customers: good and polite manners are worth having, but are noticed more when they are absent than when they are present. In other words, they are a pre-requisite.

The customer wants a product that will work and do the job he wants it to do; no amount of interpersonal competence on behalf of the supplier will detract the customer from this objective.

The key is to understand the full requirements and needs, expectations and attitudes of the customer that reflect his perception of satisfaction.

- Customer feedback is an essential management requirement.
- The customer needs and expects a friendly and effective means of inter-facing with the organization.
- It is not enough to give good service – customers must *perceive* that they are getting good service.
- The customer is not concerned with the problems facing the organization. However, if you are the customer and your supplier is failing to deliver, then to ignore the supplier's problems is not total quality. You should see if you can help your supplier to help you. If the problem continues, as a last resort, you probably have the option of changing suppliers.
- Customer loyalty can be built to a level where it is relatively durable, but it can and does change without much notice. Examples include people's tastes in fashion and food.
- Customers considering the purchase of a service will have to make judgements on factors other than the quality of the service, because unlike a tangible product the service does not yet exist. Examples include hair-dressers and travel agents.

To adopt a total quality approach you need to find out the precise benefits sought by the customer. These benefits could be one or more of the following:

- Confidentiality.
- Quality and luxury.
- Functional, inexpensive with absence of frills.
- Excitement and adventure.
- Image or status.
- Speed.
- Safety and security.
- Absence of hassle – no worries and everything taken care of.
- Flexibility.
- Specially tailored to meet specific needs.
- Special treatment like VIP, first-class, friendly, courtesy.
- Consistency and reliability.

**Customers notice when the standard of service
falls below their expectations,
but they also notice when it rises above them.**

3.4 Meeting the needs of the customer

To deliver a quality product to your customer, you must first clearly understand what it is that your customer perceives the product to be, and what his standard expectations are. When your customer has identified the standard expectations required, then – and only then – can you start to consider how you can *delight* your customer.

If your intention is just to satisfy your customer, then you are giving your competition the opportunity to offer more *delight value* in terms of their product, with the consequence that you may lose the customer.

The Royal Mail delivers, on average 67 million letters every working day, to more than 24 million addresses throughout the United Kingdom. Satisfying customers is no mean achievement. The customer's decision to use the Royal Mail again is, in part, a reflection of the service they perceive that they are getting. Independent research commissioned by Royal Mail, indicates that customers believe only 78 per cent of First Class letters are delivered the day after posting – and yet independent measurement, covering all of the United Kingdom proves that more than 93 per cent of First Class letters are actually delivered the following day.

What matters most is what the customers perceive, and not what is actually happening. The role at the Royal Mail is to continually communicate with their customers to raise perception more closely to what is happening in practice.

Quality is not just associated with a product: it is seen by the customer as the whole of the relationship. Quality is the concept the customer has about his decision to be associated with your organization. The customer is putting his own reputation and judgement on the line when he decides to take what you are offering. He expects you will honour a lifetime of support if that is necessary, otherwise he will perceive that your product is not total quality.

From an internal customer's viewpoint, your product or job function can affect his performance and career. If your deliverable is not total quality then his perception of you will, by default, be one of *not* total quality. Perhaps you are sometimes late with reports, or your work is not as accurate as it should be: perhaps you do not help when extra work comes into the office. These issues become deliverables to the internal customer and he may expect your involvement and help even though you may feel it is not your job. This is why it is important that you actively seek to understand that which your customer perceives is a standard deliverable from you. Once you understand what the standard deliverable is, then and only then can you look for things to do that will delight your customer.

Misunderstanding can be a barrier to providing a total quality approach to customer needs.

Definition of a total quality approach:
Quality is meeting the customer requirements AT ALL TIMES and
striving to exceed them whenever possible.

Royal Mail seek to avoid misunderstandings with internal customers by actively encouraging the use of quality tools and techniques that are designed to help people to work together, in a structured and consistent way.

Using this structured quality methodology minimizes misunderstandings, and both internal customers and internal suppliers, determine an agreed way forward. They ensure the external customers' requirements are the prime goal, and that they are well understood, and are consistently met.

Remember: if you supply the customer with a product that meets his standard and specification and is totally reliable and the price is right, all you have done is *satisfied* the customer. Delight for both the internal and external customer requires activities designed to make the customer positively and consciously aware of what you are doing for him over and above the standard. You must be proactive and strive to be one step ahead, not of your competition but of your customers.

Raise standards beyond those
currently expected by your customers and
deliver delight in advance of your customer expectations.

If your customer has to ask you for it, then it means he wants it as standard and it will not be a delight factor for very long. Most customers are easy to please; they simply want us to do what we say, when we say we will, consistently.

A consumer wanted to purchase a new stereo and compact disc unit. Determined to make the right choice, he spent two weekends visiting all the electrical stores in the main shopping centres in Manchester. He looked into technical specifications, price and delivery conditions, until eventually he had a comprehensive list of all the available options. Some had special offers for cash-only deals, some had zero interest payment plans, while others offered two-year service and repair guarantees. It was going to be a difficult decision.

Walking home from the railway station, the consumer passed the small electrical shop in his village. He had given the shop very little thought, perceiving that it would be expensive and lacking in range and quality options. Out of curiosity, the consumer went inside.

The manager of the shop listened carefully to his customer's requests, and then asked for what purpose the music system was needed. The consumer had not been asked questions in any of the larger shops he had visited. He told the manager that he wanted the system for a small room in his house, which he often used as an office. The consumer was then asked about his taste in music, and a few other matters in which none of the other shops had seemed remotely interested.

When the manager showed the consumer some systems which he thought were suitable, the consumer was pleasantly surprised: he would have been happy with any one of them. He told the manager that he wanted a payment plan to spread the costs over a six-month period, and the manager said that such an arrangement was fine.

The consumer decided to take a chance. Having selected a specific model, the consumer asked when it might be delivered. The manager informed him that he would deliver it himself that very evening. True to his word, he arrived on time, set up the system without a hitch, and gave the consumer three free compact discs as he left – they were by the artists the consumer had mentioned earlier that afternoon.

The consumer could have bought a cheaper unit in one of the major chain stores, but they had made no effort to make him feel special. The local store, on the other hand, had made every effort to delight their customer. His perception of the store had been totally altered, and he has now altered the perception of his acquaintances also, by talking about the total quality approach to customer care provided by the store.

3.5 Summary of customer requirements

This chapter brings together the external and internal customer, and shows that they have the same requirements and needs when it comes to delivering the *product*.

The customer determines his requirements and it is his perception only that determines whether the deliverable has satisfied his needs. Personal attitude, consistency and reliability are the main ingredients to a total quality approach. You must be proactive and continuously seek ways of improving your deliverables, adding consistent value to your product, which is of genuine advantage and benefit to your customer.

If your competition do it, then it should be part of your standard deliverable. As an internal supplier dealing with your internal customer, you should constantly seek ways of improving your internal *product*, to help increase your internal customer's productivity and contribute to the organization's main objective.

To show your customer you have listened to him is one of the greatest compliments. Make all your customers, both internal and external, feel special, valued and an important part of your business.

TEST YOUR UNDERSTANDING

The purpose of the following questions is to reinforce the issues raised in Chapter 3 and to make them relevant to each reader. Where possible discuss your answers with a colleague or better still with your department manager.

Question 1
Using the organization you work for or an organization with which you are familiar:
a) Can you identify changes to the external customer requirements that have happened over the last few years?
b) Can you identify changes to your internal customer requirements that have happened over the last few years?
c) Can you predict the changes to your external and internal customer requirements over the next five years?

Question 2
From the list of the sources of customer complaints identified in the chapter, to how many can you relate? Give at least one example of each:
a) From your external customers.
b) From your internal customers.

Question 3
Without referring back in the book, can you list as many benefits as possible that affect the customer's decision to deal with you?

Question 4
a) Make a list of all the *standard* things you would want when you book a holiday. You should list what you would expect from a good holiday organization.
b) Now make a list of all the things that would *delight* you when you book a holiday. This list should assume that your standard requirements have been met.

'If you use your skill and imagination
to see how much you can give for a dollar,
instead of how little you can give for a dollar,
you are bound to succeed.'

(Henry Ford)

CHAPTER 4

The Impact of Quality on the Business and the Customer

AIMS AND OBJECTIVES OF THIS CHAPTER

- To identify the impact of quality on the business.
- To explain the consequences of poor quality on the customer.
- To discuss the concept of the true cost of ownership.
- To define factors affecting quality.
- To encourage the reader to read Chapter 5.

4.1 The cost of quality on the business

I discussed in Chapter 2 the effects negative costs can have on the organization, and the significant positive effect that reducing negative costs can have on the financial surplus. It is these negative costs that impact the quality of the organization. These costs are associated with many different areas within the business and are divided into two main categories.

Negative Cost Category 1: Failure Costs
These are costs associated with events not being right first time. They can be reduced significantly if not eliminated. These costs add no benefit or value to the customer and have a negative effect on the financial surplus of the organization. They include:

- Scrap.
- Rework.
- Warranty repair.
- Returns.

- Downgraded items or goods.
- Write-offs.
- Shortages.
- Re-designs.
- Downtime and stoppages.

It was within these areas that Tom Peters and Charles Handy suggested that potential savings in excess of 35 per cent of operating costs existed. It is not just on the shop floor that improvements can be made but also in the administration and management areas of the business.

Negative Cost Category 2: Checking Costs
These are costs associated with processes designed to check that work carried out previously has been done correctly. They should be eliminated. These costs add no benefit or value to the customer and have a negative effect on the financial surplus of the organization. They include:

- Inspection.
- Testing.
- Proofreading.
- Checking.

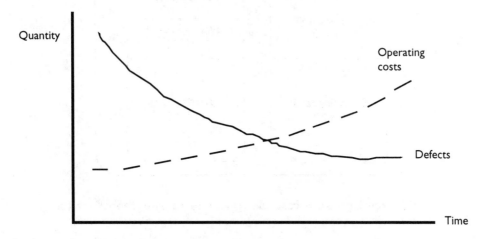

Figure 4.1: Reducing defects by increased inspection

Many organizations react to poor quality by increasing inspection and testing of the product. They increase the personnel operating these functions and increase the operating costs of the organization. This normally has the desired effect of reducing defects being shipped to the customer. However it does not stop the defects happening and it increases the costs, reduces financial surplus and hides the faults.

**Root cause analysis and elimination of the true cause of waste
is the only way to achieve quality.**

The operating costs plus the negative costs are the total costs of the organization; in the example that follows, the profits have been calculated as 10 per cent of these total costs.

The challenge for the organization is to separate the negative costs so they can be attacked and reduced or eliminated. The effect of reducing these negative costs has an immediate and significant effect on the financial surplus of the organization. In the example to follow, reducing the negative costs by 50 per cent will increase the financial surplus by over 160 per cent. This increase in the financial surplus (profit) is equivalent to a two-and-a-half-times increase in turnover.

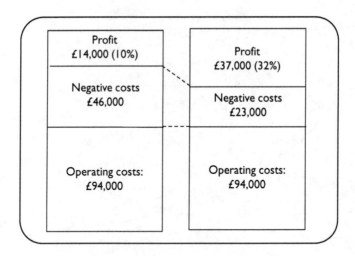

Figure 4.2: Reducing negative costs can significantly increase financial surplus

This model is a very powerful communicating tool to show the impact of a total quality approach throughout an organization. It is important that the identification and measurement of the negative costs are carried out in a quality way.

The way to approach the reduction and elimination of negative costs is by implementing a programme of *prevention costs*. These are positive pro-grammes that address:

- Training.
- Education.
- Preventative maintenance.
- Process improvement.
- Effective procedures.
- Effective measures.
- Regular audits.

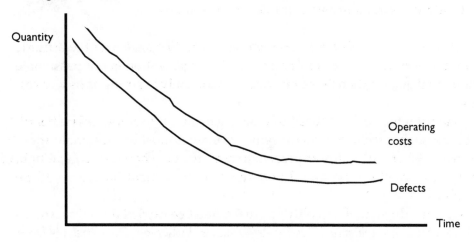

Figure 4.3: Reducing defects by root cause prevention

Defects should be prevented from occurring by removing their causes, and not through inspection. Removing the causes of the defects ensures that the defects do not reoccur. Doing it right first time costs less than doing it again.

A formula for the Cost of Quality (C.O.Q.) is:

C. O. Q. = Failure Cost + Inspection Cost + Prevention Cost

It is often not the circumstances or situations that occur, which cause the problem – it is our reactions.

Education and training will never be as expensive as ignorance.

4.2   Factors affecting quality in the business

A total quality approach is all about people and their interaction inside and outside the business. It is people who are responsible for most of the defects. Like all assets of the business, people need maintenance. The maintenance of people is the key to a total quality approach.

There are three primary factors affecting a total quality approach:

- Attitude.
- Informed and timely communication.
- Continuous training and improved qualifications.

Attitude is the single most important factor affecting quality. If the attitude from the very top to the very bottom of the organization is not passionate about total quality, then the organization will be only as strong as its weakest link.

Quality must be introduced into an organization top-down. The board, the managing director and all the senior managers must be passionate about the need for a total quality approach. If they are not, when things get tough, root causes will not be found and short-cut expedient answers will be sought.

The introduction of a quality approach must be carried out with care, as this extract from *Achieving Quality Performance*[1] indicates. The extract is from a study of the Prudential Corporation plc and shows:

A number of obstacles have been overcome since 1989 and lessons have been learnt. For some staff, the cultural shift that has taken place has been difficult to cope with and as a result they have left the organization. With any change there will be a degree of resistance from some individuals and it is very important that this is dealt with effectively by management. It is obviously much easier to introduce a TQM programme into a new or young business than into one which is restricted by many years of established procedures and tasks.

The time taken to 'roll out' a change programme is crucial – too quickly can mean that the details are not fully understood, and too slowly can result in a loss of momentum.

Training staff is a sensitive task and attention needs to be given to ensuring that the 'pitch' of the material meets the requirements of the target audience and does not underestimate or overestimate their abilities. In addition, the language used must be meaningful and related to the particular needs of each department.

At Prudential, the establishment of working groups consisting of a cross-section of employees, placed managers in a vulnerable position where they could be questioned and challenged by more junior members of staff. It is therefore very important that managers are well prepared for their role in the TQM system.

If the change is not made with care, the disadvantages may well outweigh the benefits.

Consider the following statement and reflect on its implications.

**'Is the answer to the problem,
the same as the solution to the problem?'**

Complementing the three primary factors affecting quality are many supporting factors such as:

- Clear specifications.
- Good meaningful procedures.
- Excellent communication system within the organization and outside the organization.
- Effective and well-maintained equipment throughout the organization.
- Effective research and development.
- Effective marketing.
- Effective financial controls.
- Effective materials management.

4.3 The cost of quality to the customer

When a customer deals with a supplier for a product he has a perceived standard view of the quality expected. If this standard of quality is not received, then the effect and the cost of this disappointment can take the form of:

- a feeling of irritation;
- a sense of frustration;
- anger, stemming from a feeling of having been cheated;
- loss of face for the customer, and a permanent doubt over his judgement in choosing a supplier.

These negative costs are all due to non-quality deliverables. The impact on the customer does not stop there. Actual customers interact and communicate with potential customers. A Gallup survey from 1992 indicated that every dissatisfied customer will tell an average of eleven acquaintances about the problems he has experienced.

Customer complaints do not always relate to the quality of the service or product, but to peripheral issues like colour, packaging, or instruction booklet. Quality, in the eyes of the customer, is always more than the quality of the physical product. The customer sees quality as not one thing, but a series of deliverables such as:

- product reliability;
- consistency;
- speed and timeliness of delivery;
- accuracy of paperwork;
- courtesy on the telephone;
- value of information given;
- reputation;
- positive attitude by staff.

All these elements are important and some are critical. The only reliable way to find out which elements are critical to your customers is to seek positive opportunities to encourage your customers to tell you.

4.4 Factors affecting quality for the customer

Research from the Forum Corporation in the USA shows that over 40 per cent of customers will take their business to the competition because of poor quality. The poor quality can be related to the product, but in many cases it is poor quality customer relationships that lose customers.

Some companies have realized that customers who take their business elsewhere are not only damaging to reputation (because they will spread the word), but they also cost a great deal of money (because attracting a new customer to replace the old one is expensive). These companies try to ensure that customers are persuaded to stay on, whatever the circumstances.

The following extract from, *Service Quality in Hospitality Organizations*[2] illustrates this point:

> While it is possible to make mistakes in any service firm, it is fundamental and essential to commit to service recovery. Hart *et al* (1990) discuss how the best companies turn complaining customers into loyal ones. The case of Club Med-Cacun provides a good example. Recovery is fundamental to service excellence and should therefore be regarded as an integral part of a service company's strategy. It is perhaps five times more expensive to replace a customer than it is to retain one. At Club Med, one lost customer costs the company at least $2,400, plus the high cost of marketing efforts to find a replacement (Hart *et al*, 1990). Given the cost, companies should take steps to ensure that employees have the skill, motivation and authority to make service recovery an integral part of operations. Some successful techniques for developing service recovery skills can be developed through simulated real-life situations and role playing. Sonesta Hotels uses games as part of its orientation program for new employees, so as to enhance their service skills.

Those organizations which concentrate resources on customer retention are likely to save money in the long run.

If an organization responds quickly to a customer complaint or a problem, then over 80 per cent of those customers will continue doing business with the organization. Loyalty increases if you respond instantly. By responding instantly, the quality organization is sending a message to its customer that customers are important, and the organization listens to them. This is a very powerful message.

The main factors that affect quality in the eyes of the customer are:

- Uncaring employees.
- Poor employee training.
- Negative attitudes of employees towards customers.
- Differences in perception between:
  - what the business thinks the customer needs and what the customer wants;
  - the product or service the business thinks it provides and what the customer thinks he actually receives;
  - the way the business thinks the customer wants to be treated, and the way the customer really wants to be treated.
- No customer service philosophy within the company.
- Poor handling and resolution of complaints.
- Employees are not empowered to provide good service, and have to seek permission or guidance.
- Poor treatment of employees as customers.

The statistics shown in Figure 4.4 represent an increase of over 1,400 per cent in financial surplus over five years. This is an astounding achievement and a clear indication of what can be done through adopting a quality approach.

Royal Mail financial surplus (profit) since embracing the total quality approach

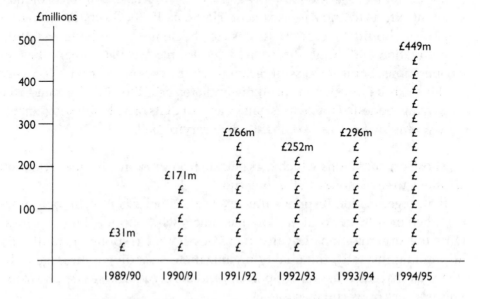

Figure 4.4: Financial justification for adopting a quality approach

4.5 Cost of ownership

Customers deal with organizations for five main reasons: these are known as the buying enablers and can act as a competitive advantage if your product can deliver the benefit to the customer. The five main reasons why a customer takes a product are:

1. *To save money* (choosing Kwiksave over Marks & Spencer).
2. *To save time* (choosing the village shop over the nearest supermarket).
3. *To feel secure* (choosing double-glazed windows over period windows).
4. *To improve self-esteem* (choosing a designer shirt over a generic one).
5. *To enjoy leisure time* (choosing a computer game over a software package).

When a customer procures the product, the price he pays is just the beginning of the relationship. The customer will judge the quality of the product by the cost of using it over its lifetime.

The cost of buying a car may initially be the price you pay to the showroom. However the true cost of the car is the purchase price plus costs associated with: buying the road tax; buying the insurance; running costs for petrol and oil; service costs; repair costs.

In some instances the cost of not buying or doing something because you have bought the car is part of the cost of owning that product. Perhaps you did not go abroad on holiday for two years because you could not afford to pay for the car and have a foreign holiday. This action was all part of procuring the car, therefore the true cost or the *cost of ownership* was greater than just a financial calculation: *cost of ownership* frequently involves an emotion or sacrifice.

It is essential that the organization recognizes this element, as it can be one of the most powerful influences over why customers do or do not buy your products.

Identifying the true cost (cost of ownership) of your product is critical if you want to be successful and deliver quality. Understanding the customer's cost of owning your product can focus attention on how to add more value and increase your customer expectations thus increasing the need for the customer to deal with you.

**The cost of ownership is the true cost of any product
and the organization that delivers the best value in terms of ownership
will have a competitive advantage over its rivals.**

4.6 Summary of the impact of quality

This chapter established that the cost of quality on the business can be identified in three ways:

- Failure costs: these are costs that are associated *with not doing it right first time.*
- Checking costs: these are costs associated with having to *check you did it right first time.*
- Prevention costs: those costs that are incurred to *help you do it right first time.*

Clearly, by skilful management of these costs significant improvements can be made to the financial surplus of the organization.

To achieve these savings three primary factors affecting a total quality approach were identified and some enabling supporting factors were listed. These illustrate the difficulties of introducing a structured quality approach. They reinforce the important message that a quality approach is not a quick fix, nor does it have an end: it is an everlasting journey of continuous improvement with training and education as its primary focus.

Attitude was identified as the single most important factor affecting quality: this is the attitude of employees to customer needs, requirements and expectations.

The question *'Is the answer to the problem the same as the solution to the problem?'* was asked. It is hoped that the reader has thought through the significance of this question and concluded that answers can be quick fixes, whereby solutions need time, understanding, analysis and informed discussion with supporting data.

A total quality approach is the *solution* to increased financial surplus and continued growth in today's demanding and competitive environment.

The reader should now be realizing that there is not one answer or simple formula to introduce a total quality approach into any organization. Each organization is different: the people are different and the needs, visions and expectations are different; this was highlighted by identifying some of the customer issues. Customer emotions have a major impact on motivation to deal with any particular organization, and the value of quality as perceived by the customer is greater than the sum of specific single quality actions.

The true cost of the product sold by organizations is known as the cost of ownership and is a very important part of understanding the total quality approach.

TEST YOUR UNDERSTANDING

The purpose of the following questions is to reinforce the issues raised in Chapter 4 and to make them relevant to each reader. Where possible discuss your answers with a colleague or better still your department manager.

Question 1
Use the organization you work in or an organization with which you are familiar to answer this question.
a) Failure costs are not just associated with manufacturing, they occur in all job roles. Identify some of the failure costs associated with your own job role.
b) Identify some of the *checking costs* associated with your own job.
c) Can you identify any *preventative costs* associated with your own job?

Question 2
From your answers in Question 1 you should now attempt to put a monetary value on the failure, checking and prevention costs identified.

Question 3
How many of the supporting factors affecting quality are present in your organization? Make a list and identify the reason why you think they exist.

Question 4
From the list of factors affecting quality as perceived by the customer, how many can you identify existing in your organization?

Question 5
Can you identify the cost of ownership relating to your product for all the different types of customer who deal with your organization?

Notes to Chapter 4
1. *Achieving Quality Performance*, edited by Richard Teare, Cyril Atkinson and Clive Westwood. London: Cassell, 1994; p. 167.
2. *Service Quality in Hospitality Organisations*, edited by Richard Teare, Michael D. Olsen and Evert Gummesson. London: Cassell, 1996; p. 303.

CHAPTER 5

How to Delight Your Customer

AIMS AND OBJECTIVES OF THIS CHAPTER

- To explain the need to encourage customers to provide feedback.

- To show ways of encouraging customers to provide feedback.

- To draw attention to the difficulties in measuring customer feedback.

- To identify ways of overcoming the problems of measuring customer feedback.

- To suggest a starting point to implement a total quality approach.

- To encourage the reader to read Chapter 6.

5.1 Encourage feedback

You should try to form partnerships with your customers: genuine open alliances that encourage frank and honest exchanges of ideas and suggestions. A wise organization – or in the case of an internal customer, a wise worker – will use information from customers as a means to improve and possibly excel.

You can encourage customers to help you improve your business or job role, and provide a better product by asking them to give you feedback. Encourage them to tell you how you can make things easier or better for them. Positively encourage your customers to tell you when they do not like something. Be prepared for this knowledge, as it may not be pleasant for you to hear – but if you can respond positively to the challenge, it will greatly increase your financial surplus.

Do not always expect the customer to know how to improve something; most customers may only tell you that something is a problem, they may not know the answer.

The best way to delight your customer is to find out what he thinks. This can be achieved by asking some straightforward questions:

- Who are your customers?
- When are they your customers?
- Why are they your customers?
- What do they want?
- How do they feel?
- How can you make your customers feel valued?
- What initiatives would your customers appreciate?

From the answers to these questions you could ask:

- What can you do to keep your customers?
- How can you give yourself a customer competitive edge?

You need to ask, and receive answers to, these fundamental questions regularly. If you do not take the time to find out about your customer, either because you cannot be bothered or because you think you already know, you may find that you are taken by surprise when your customers go elsewhere.

**If you do not know why somehing is happening
you will not concentrate your efforts on the corrective action.
If you think you know why it is happening, but you are wrong,
then any action you take will be misguided.**

When you have listened carefully to your customer, it is essential that you demonstrate positively that you have responded to his needs. You may only be able to respond in a small way to start with – but this is very powerful as it shows the customer you value him. Customers who feel special, who feel valued, who know they are listened to, inevitably continue dealing with the organization. By listening hard and responding positively, you are making the customer feel like a partner in your business. Getting customers to be partners in your organization makes a strong emotional bond, and emotions build loyalty.

Ways to encourage feedback:

- Make it easy for customers to complain.
- Seek out customers at random and ask for their comments.
- Learn not to be defensive when listening to complaints.
- Act quickly to resolve problems.

- Replace defective products immediately.
- Take positive steps to eliminate a complaint to stop reoccurrence.
- Be creative and devise ways of actively seeking feedback.

This process should be as natural as you can make it. You should not make customer feedback a special occasion – it should be part of your everyday activity.

**Consistent and continuous feedback
allows consistent and continuous improvement.**

5.2 Why measuring customer feedback is difficult

There are many dangers involved in measuring and analyzing customer feedback:

- Perhaps only dissatisfied customers give you feedback. This could mean that all those customers who are satisfied or delighted with your product never tell you.
- Relying on customer complaints as a measure of customer satisfaction means that all you do is respond to negatives. Perhaps some customers would never complain, because they feel you would not do anything about it anyhow. They have no confidence in your organization to respond to their needs. This kind of customer will take his business else-where as soon as the opportunity arises. They are not emotionally attached to your organization.
- If the feedback from customers was from a specific time period, then this historic analysis may not represent what is happening in the business today.
- Perhaps you have so many customers due to the nature of your business that you only solicit feedback from your major accounts, or from highly articulate customers. The danger here is that you may set your strategy on the back of a customer who has not listened to his customers – he may have it wrong. Remember, many of your customers will not have a total quality approach to their business.
- Customer feedback may be collected correctly, but no one may regard the results as meaningful.
- The organization may have a preconceived idea about its customers and may consider it knows what is best. The attitude may be that if it is not broken, there is no need to fix it.

5.3 How to overcome the problems associated with customer feedback

Here are some powerful questions you should regularly ask your customers (remember there are two types of customer, internal and external).

External customer:
- Did the product you received today meet with your expectations? If not, what went wrong?
- If there is one thing you would like to see us improve, what would it be?
- How can we earn more of your business?

Internal customer:
- Did the product you received today meet with your expectations? If not, what went wrong?
- If there is one thing you would like to see us improve, what would it be?
- How can I make your job more effective?

To complement the questions and to generally seek feedback in a positive and active way you should consider some of the ideas listed below:

- Telephone surveys.
- Face-to-face interviews.
- Form customer task force groups (MG Club, Lego Club, Star Trek Club).
- Instal a freephone number.
- Commission a third-party survey.

To check what products or service your customers receive try pretending to be a customer and contact your organization, and order the product or service. How did it feel – were you disappointed, satisfied, or delighted? Allocate a senior manager, from a non-customer contact function in the organization, to shadow and interface with the process of customer contact and delivery.

Royal Mail continues to develop a consistent, high specification level of response to all of its customers who contact the organization over the telephone. Linked to the standards laid down in the Citizens Charter, Royal Mail North Wales North West Division undertakes a Mystery Shopper exercise, by telephoning to all of its 250 delivery offices.

The Mystery Shopper exercise measures: speed of response (how quickly was the telephone answered); knowledge (an in-depth question to establish the employees' knowledge of either a product or service specification); quality and courtesy (how polite and courteous was the greeting and the way that the telephone call was handled).

This data is collected and fed back to the respective delivery offices as a means of stimulating improvement against the three aspects that are measured. This provides the opportunity for further training as required and also gives recognition to those people in the offices that are identified as doing particularly well.

5.4 How to instil a total quality approach

Every journey must start with one step. The total quality approach is a journey that will last a lifetime and must be undertaken by every person. For an organization to succeed, the journey must be made with the leader of the organization (managing director) and all his reportees leading from the front. They must show a clear and unfaltering commitment and passion for the aims and objectives of a total quality approach to increased financial surplus. The steps to be undertaken are, first, to talk, talk, talk about the benefits of a total quality approach to the business. Second, undertake an awareness programme. This does not have to be expensive or involve consultants. Suggestions to consider:

- Several local institutions may be able to help you. You could try your nearest university, or a college of further education. Other places to consider include professional institutes, Chambers of Commerce, and public libraries.
- Enquire in your area if there are any Total Quality Forum business meetings. This is a regular get-together of businesses who are at various stages on the TQA journey. They meet on a regular basis and help each other. It is called Benchmarking. Organizations take the best practices from other organizations and try to implement them in their own business. This eliminates the need to keep making the same mistakes or reinvent the wheel.
- Contact some of the other organizations in your area and see what they are doing. If they have started the TQA journey they will probably be delighted to come and talk to you, or better still let you go to talk to them.

From this point on, every organization is different and there is no formula that is right for every business. However, if the senior managers have come this far they will be convinced that TQA will improve their business significantly, and they must decide how they will proceed.

Some strategies to follow
- Create a total quality approach as part of your culture.
- Have a mission statement that is communicated to all.
- Have company objectives that are communicated to all.
- Involve everyone, including the cleaning staff.
- Put all procedures in writing, but keep them simple and readable so they will be used.

- Empower the employees to deliver quality to the customer at all levels.
- Train, train, train and continue to train all employees.
- Communicate to the outside world that you embrace a total quality approach to your customers.
- Recruit good people – have a positive policy of recruiting quality people for a quality company.
- Measure your quality and put a value on it. Use the TQA tools and techniques.
- Continuously empower your people to set improved standards.
- Provide job rotation.
- Be proactive and educate your customers in a total quality approach.
- Turn complaints into opportunities for increased business.
- Instil a *'right first time'* attitude and support, recognize and reward those who embrace it. Remember, we learn more from trying and failing than from not trying at all.
- Treat every customer with a lifetime value.
- Be proactive and encourage customer feedback.
- Encourage employee involvement and suggestions.
- Be fair and consistent.
- Under-promise and over-deliver.
- Compete on quality benefits to the customer, not on price.
- Know the cost of losing a customer.
- Know your competition.
- Do regular market surveys.
- Communicate, communicate, communicate.
- Remember internal customers have a significant effect on financial surplus.
- Let customers know you care.

As an individual, you should not let the fact that your neighbour, colleague or boss does not have a total quality approach stop you. *'If he is not doing it, I am not doing it'* – that is a no-win situation. Give yourself the opportunity of adding real value and meaning, not only to your working life, but to your personal life, by embracing the messages and principles of a total quality approach. This will add personal value to *'your product'* and will give you the chance to reach your full potential.

If you have not got time to do it right,
when will you have time to do it again?

5.5 Summary of how to delight your customer

Encouraging your customer to talk to you about your product is an essential part of continuous improvement. This process must be seen as a genuine attempt to improve, and there must be some tangible changes implemented as soon as possible after the feedback. Remember that listening to your customer without positive action, is the same as ignoring your customer.

This does not imply that everything the customer says he wants is possible, or indeed something that you want to give. But you must make positive replies to your customer's suggestions and problems, and if you are unable to implement their requirements then you must communicate your reasons clearly.

Always make it easy for customers to complain and make listening a natural part of your everyday role.

Consider that when a customer owes an organization money, most organizations will chase the customer until payment is made. If a customer stops doing business with the organization, most organizations do nothing. *Why?*

Measuring your customer feedback (even negative feedback), is important to demonstrate improvements over time. This is not always easy, and the understanding and use of total quality approach tools and techniques is essential. Part Two of this book will introduce some of the primary tools needed to fulfil this process. You should always remember that customers are external and internal and their treatment should be the same.

Instilling a total quality approach attitude is the start of a long journey that will be difficult in places, frustrating and challenging. It can, however, be very rewarding both for the organization and for the individuals involved. The main criteria for success are: communicate; communicate; communicate.

If you are not thinking about a total quality approach and your competitors are, then you are already behind in the race for customers. This is not a fad or the latest management buzz-phrase, it is a realistic and proven way to run a successful, strong, and growing business – ask the Japanese.

It was Charles Handy who said that the status quo will no longer be the best way forward. So if you agree that what you are doing at the moment is not the best you can do, then you must agree that you will have to change or the business will die. If you are going to make changes, then make them with success in mind and take the path that leads to *a quality approach.*

In the words of Peter Drucker and Tom Peters:

**'Know what you are, what you can do
and keep focused on improvements by being proactive,
listen and invest in people through training and education.'**

TEST YOUR UNDERSTANDING

The purpose of the following questions is to reinforce the issues raised in Chapter 5 and to make them relevant to each reader. Where possible discuss your answers with a colleague or better still your department manager.

Question 1
Using an organization you work in or an organization with which you are familiar:
a) Identify ways in which the organization encourages external customers to feed back information on the product.
b) Identify ways in which you encourage your internal customers to feed back information on the product you deliver to them.

Question 2
Using an organization you work in or an organization with which you are familiar:
a) Identify the barriers to collecting regular feedback from your external customer.
b) Identify the barriers to collecting regular feedback from your internal customer.

Question 3
How could you implement a customer feedback process, (or improve your existing one) for:
a) Your organizational external customers?
b) Your personal internal customers?

CHAPTER 6

The Seven Primary Organizational Cultures

AIMS AND OBJECTIVES OF THIS CHAPTER

- To introduce the primary organizational cultures existing in the Western business world.

- To describe these cultures in a simple and informative way so the reader can identify specific characteristics and recognize these traits in organizations with which he is familiar.

- To encourage the reader to read Part Two of this book.

6.1 Corporate culture

It is necessary to distinguish between the *formal* and *informal* aspects of corporate culture. Formal values are outlined in mission and vision statements, procedures and other formal control systems. Sometimes these formal values operate as little more than a public relations smoke screen, behind which the organization behaves quite differently.

Formal values will only be meaningful if they are supported by the right informal culture. These informal values develop over time and are shaped by such factors as:

- The extent and manner of senior management involvement.
- The degree to which senior management practise leadership by example and act as a positive role model to customer service.
- The consistency with which customer-care policies are implemented.
- The commitment of middle management.
- The existence of reward systems and recognition systems for customer service.
- The myths and stories that circulate within the organization about past practices and current priorities.

It is usually these informal values that determine the true measure of an organization's strategies towards its business and customers. It is important that there are no doubts or uncertainties about implementation, or anxiety about its outcome.

Charles Handy, in his book *Understanding Organisations*, suggests four types of culture: Task; Person; Role; Power. I would like to propose an extension of Handy's cultures by building on his work and introducing three new types: the *Balanced* culture; the *Shared* culture; and the *Mature* culture.

6.2 Task culture

- Maximum concerns for production: minimum concerns for people.
- Individual and group concern for results is primary, people are secondary. The resulting operational culture is likely to be one of conflict, one-upmanship, antagonism, competition and criticism.
- Goals and objectives are established by the boss with little or no consultation. The norms and standards are primarily a reflection of the boss's attitude towards team performance and the boss's definition of acceptable behaviour.
- Jobs are assigned by the boss. There are rigid lines of authority, and co-ordination among members is low.
- Feedback consists mostly of fault-finding and criticism when things go wrong. Morale and cohesion are low. There is frequent antagonism towards the company.
- Win-lose environment.
- Territorial rights and low co-operation among members.

This type of culture does not encourage genuine customer feedback and involvement, as it would interfere with the running of the organization. Customers are probably seen as problems rather than opportunities.

6.3 Person culture

- Minimum concern for production: maximum concern for people.
- Fostering good feelings takes precedence over operational results. The team's primary concern is with rewards and benefits, working conditions, comfort, friendliness and avoidance of conflict.
- The boss is likely to be a friend rather than a leader. This situation could avoid controversial issues that may generate conflict and cause bad feelings.
- Goals and objectives are geared towards individuals retaining harmony rather than towards the productive purpose of the team. However, the team is likely to be satisfied with its outputs.
- Norms and standards in a people culture permit the satisfaction, personal convenience, and whims of team members to prevail over issues of productivity that would interfere with these concerns.
- Job assignments are based on expressed personal preferences, rather than demonstrated competence.
- Feedback is concerned with emphasising positive aspects of performance while downplaying or ignoring problems.
- Morale is generally high, but it comes from a sense of team members being nice to each other, rather than from positive feelings that come from true accomplishment or performance.

Customer complaints can be channelled in this environment, but if the feedback is not what people would like to hear, it will not be encouraged. Problems will be ignored or blamed on circumstances, they will not be seen as opportunities.

6.4 Role culture

- Single focused: concerns are high for both results and people, but not at the same time.
- The two concerns are not integrated: a high concern for production is followed by a high concern for people. This style is leader- or organization-orientated with strong control. There are rewards for compliance, and criticism or rejection for non-compliance. Members are obedient for a price.
- The authority is firmly with the boss. The goals and objectives are the boss's. People are expected to comply and they are rewarded when they do.
- Job assignments are to ensure the boss's direction and control and heighten the member's dependence on the boss.
- Feedback is viewed in a negative way as undermining the boss.
- Morale can be high, particularly during periods of success. However, members can become frustrated under this culture when they want to try something new, as it may seem that they are disloyal.

This environment runs hot and cold regarding customer feedback. If it suits the moment, action will be taken in a totally focused way – but then over time, something else will become more important and the customer issues will be relegated down the priority list.

6.5 Power culture

- Several styles are used interchangeably, depending on the person involved.
- The motives are to be on top, to be Number One, but the objectives are self-orientated, rather than organizational. Empire-building and career enhancement interests take precedence over the team results.
- Power and authority are seen as a means to attain personal ends. The team's goals and objectives are extensions of the personal goals of the members. As such, the objectives are frequently to gain power and control in relation to other teams, rather than to further organizational productivity.
- Norms and standards with respect to performance may be high on the surface, but they are set in competition, with political meaning, and are best characterized as devious and unprincipled.
- Assignments are determined by the boss on the basis of whose work can most effectively enhance his reputation. There is competition for assignments which carry a perceived importance, and back-door methods are often used to gain acceptance.
- Feedback consists of praise and compliments in public, with criticism and backbiting in private.
- It is all about advancing one's own interests.
- Morale and cohesion will be up and down with the moment.

This environment is highly political. Individuals and departments compete and co-operate for power and all decisions are evaluated for their relative impact on the power structure. The leader is dominant. Customers can sometimes get in the way of personal opportunities. Customer feedback is highly filtered and usually superficial. Workers will put themselves out for customers if it means scoring personal points or gaining some sort of credit within the organization.

6.6 Balanced culture

- Average amounts of concern for production and people.
- Team members resort to rules and policies in order to minimize conflict and ensure acceptability and conformity to the organization and to each member.
- Leadership is based on accepting the status quo with a little movement towards progress without losing any ground. If disagreements arise, they are dealt with through compromise, and not direct confrontation.
- Procedures, rules and systems are employed not so much to organize people, but to control them, keep them in step and settle arguments with them when conflict arises.
- Goals and objectives are likely to be short-term, based off the past and aimed at maximizing the present situation. They will not be looking very far into the future, nor will there be any strategic long-term plans.
- Norms and standards are likely to be expressed as doing better than last year or being above average. Progress is measured in terms of what has been, not what could be.
- Assignments are shared. There is little personal judgement needed in the job. Feedback tends to be superficial.
- It is *who* you know, not *what* you know. Politics are played. Being even-tempered and willing to compromise are regarded as essential qualities in this culture.

In this environment reaction to customer feedback usually exists on an historic basis. The organization does not proactively seek change through customer participation. It will compromise and put itself out for customers when it needs to, but this will be the exception rather than the rule.

6.7 Shared culture

- Minimum concern exists for both production and people.
- Survival becomes the mode of the team, and responses are calculated to ensure compliance with orders and objectives. Self-protection, individuality, low tolerance for risk are likely to be the cultural norm.
- The boss may have little more than a title. Such a boss becomes isolated from daily pressure and exerts little influence on communication, coordination or decision-making.
- In the shared culture, goals and objectives are rarely generated. Direction comes from outside the team through instructions, and members respond by meeting the minimum requirements for performance. Norms and standards are more likely to have been established by neglect or accident, rather than by intention. Therefore standards of performance are at the lowest level that the organization can tolerate.
- Assignments are likely to reflect availability rather than talent or competence. Job priorities are only established to relieve pressures from outside the team, otherwise members do the least demanding job.
- Feedback is minimal. Shortcomings and problems are ignored, unless they are very serious. Members are expected to look after their own responsibilities, and feedback from others is neither expected nor welcomed.

In this environment, customer feedback may be the flavour of the month or it may not. This organization is reactive, and not proactive. Employees in such a culture are likely to shirk responsibility, deny problems exist, and do their jobs without thinking.

6.8 Mature culture

- Both production and people concerns are fully integrated at a high level in a team approach. The team and its members are goal-orientated and seek results by participation, involvement and commitment of all those who can contribute.
- The boss stimulates others to become involved in the problems and committed to solutions, through shared participation. Each team member has a say in the outcome and feels responsible both for the team task and the individual activities.
- Goals and objectives are based on standards of excellence and are geared to increasing the involvement and ownership of those responsible for achieving them. People willingly contribute and buy in to the tasks.
- Norms and standards are based on mutual understanding and commitment among team members and are established by agreeing conditions that will allow excellent performance. These standards do not happen by accident: they are created by intent and become norms by conscious effort. Team members hold one another accountable for performance that meets these standards.
- Structured problem-solving tools and techniques are used, and members' skills are fully utilized. Assignments are used to train less competent members with opportunities for developing and learning through others.
- Feedback is candid and open and used to examine team performance and lessons to be learned. Everyone is encouraged to look at the process and not the person.
- Morale is positive, with a feeling of involvement.
- There is a high degree of trust among team members, who find many ways to support one another.

This type of organization is *rare* but it does exist. It is totally customer-focused and encourages internal and external feedback. It has a visible, open process of communicating all feedback to every member of the organization and it actively encourages all stakeholders to contribute and participate in continuous improvement and strategy formulation.

6.9 Summary of organizational cultures

The culture of an organization reflects its values and standards. There are eight factors that go to make up an organization's culture. They are:

1. *Styles of decision-making.* Are they dictatorial or participative?
2. *Objectives.* Do objectives exist? Are they in writing? Are they communicated? Are they shared?
3. *Competitive advantage.* Does the organization know what its competitive advantage is? Has it got one? Is it communicated throughout the organization? Is it invested in and valued?
4. *Organizational structure.* Is it hierarchical or is it a flat, lean horizontal structure? Is it customer focused?
5. *Management systems.* Do they exist? Are they computerized? Are they open or closed? Is it a burden to the workers and organization, or an asset? Is it customer focused?
6. *Management of people.* Is it autocratic or participative? Do effective recognition and reward systems exist? Do people feel valued?

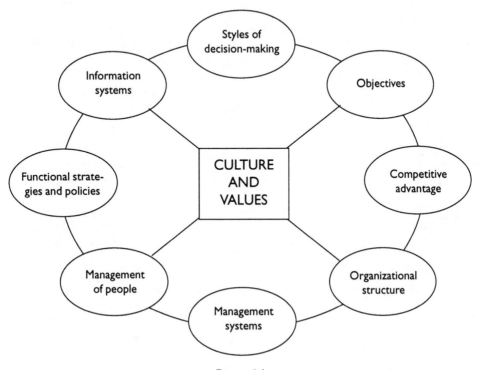

Figure 6.1

7. *Functional strategies and policy.* Do they exist? Are they communicated to all employees? Are they agreed and shared?
8. *Information systems.* Are they open and shared by all? Are there opportunities for questions? Is the information produced on time? Is the information relevant? Does it add value to the customer? Does it add value to the product? Does it add value to the organization?

A total quality approach to the enabling factors shown in Figure 6.1 will help an organization adapt to change and reach its full potential. However, this will only be possible through its people and the involvement of all the organizational stakeholders.

**To change,
it is first necessary to be aware that there is something better.**

TEST YOUR UNDERSTANDING

The purpose of the following questions is to reinforce the issues raised in Chapter 6 and to make them relevant to each reader. Where possible discuss your answers with a colleague or better still your department manager.

Question 1
a) In what type of cultural organization do you currently work?
b) In what type of cultural organization would you like to work?

Question 2
Can you afford not to improve?

Question 3
If the answer to Question 2 was 'No', then read Part Two and learn about the primary quality tools and techniques.

If the answer to Question 2 was 'Yes' then go back to the beginning of the book and start reading Chapter 1.

CHAPTER 7

A Summary of Part One

Every business and organization is a process – it has inputs (suppliers), processes (tasks) and then outputs (customers). Within this overall organizational model, there are many more detailed activities that are the result of inputs, processes and outputs. These are all the tasks and roles performed by the stakeholders of the organization. This model can be completed for every person working in an organization and for every task undertaken within an organization.

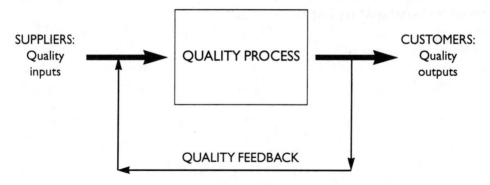

Figure 7.1: The quality approach model

A quality approach starts with an understanding of the elements that influence this model:

- reasons for the organization/function/task;
- the internal customer/supplier;
- the external customer/supplier;
- the expected inputs (requirements and perceptions);
- the expected outputs (requirements and perceptions);
- the factors affecting quality inputs and quality outputs;
- the methods of communicating feedback and results.

By understanding Part One of this book, you should be able to reproduce this model in detail for all your activities.

- Start by identifying all the processes within your area of responsibility (or organization) at the highest level first of all, then move down into increasing detail as you progress.
- By looking at each process, identify what the quality outputs are.
- Then determine what should be seen or perceived as quality outputs.
- Next, analyze the inputs into the process. How do they affect the process? Are they part of the problem? Do they complement the quality output(s) requirements?
- Now examine the process and identify the waste and failure elements that negate the quality output(s) required.
- Then determine how you record and measure the output(s), encourage and communicate feedback.

A process does not just mean a mechanical or machine-based activity. There is a great deal of waste in the support functions throughout most organizations. These support functions are processes that need continuous improvement and perpetual focusing on customer needs.

Remember that every time you change one thing in your organization there will be a change in something else. This *cause and effect* phenomenon is an important aspect of change and continuous improvement. Of course, not all these unseen changes will necessarily be positive or good. Some improvements may only uncover other hidden problems. That is why this perpetual and continuous drive for quality is a lifelong journey and not a destination.

Adopting a quality approach to everything you do has these benefits:

- *Improves quality:* by consistently analyzing and removing failure within the processes of the organization.
- *Reduces cost:* by consistently analyzing and removing waste within the processes of the organization.
- *Improves reliability:* by consistently analyzing and improving the processes of the organization.
- *Improves customer perception:* by consistently encouraging customer feedback.
- *Promotes teamwork:* by consistently involving and promoting stakeholder participation and involvement.
- *Provides a competitive edge:* by consistently focusing on key customers and organizational strengths.

- *Improves attitudes:* by consistently focusing on the customer, the organizational processes and the financial surplus.
- *Improves the working environment:* by consistently recognizing and rewarding quality initiatives.

There is not one all-embracing way of implementing a quality approach. Each organization is unique and the critical issues will vary; *but,* more importantly, the people will all be different. A quality approach is more about the attitude of the people than a prescriptive formulated routine.

To make quality improvements you now need to read Part Two to acquire understanding and skills in the primary quality tools . This will enable you to plan and monitor the effective quality changes in your organization.

Part Two

CHAPTER 8

Consensus Analytical Tools and Techniques

AIMS AND OBJECTIVES OF THIS CHAPTER

- To show a powerful and structured way to solve problems, set up effective measures and control the management of change.

- To explain the use of some powerful quality tools and techniques which will assist the reader in the challenge and drive for continuous improvement inherent in using a quality approach to work.

- To improve and extend the reader's knowledge.

THE FUTURE INVADES THE PRESENT

The need for continuous improvement

Man has traded since before 6000 BC. It is trade that has separated humans from the animal kingdom, and it is trade that has driven development, domination and expectation. Consider that some of the main factors of trading success were, and still are:

- the ability to communicate accurately, quickly, and effectively;
- the ability to transport information, goods and people accurately, quickly, and effectively;
- the ability to create needs accurately, quickly and effectively.

The development of trade can be plotted in line with the improvements in communication and transportation over the last 8,000 years.

Considering the total time human beings have been trading, the improvements and changes that have taken place in the last 250 years are astounding.

Half of the energy used in the last 2,000 years has been consumed in the last 100 years. In 1850, there were fewer than six cities in the world with a population greater than one million people; in 1950, there were over 120 cities throughout the world with populations greater than one million; in 1994, there are over 160 cities throughout the world with populations greater than one million. The spread of large cities has been extraordinarily rapid.

The time it takes to bring a product from conception to production has decreased equally quickly. For example, the first English patent for a typewriter was issued in 1714, but it was the 1860s before they were commercially available. The vacuum cleaner, electric oven and refrigerator were introduced in the 1920s but it took until the 1950s before they were in mass production (the Second World War had some influence on this delay). Televisions and automatic washing machines were being produced in the 1940s and 1950s, but it took less than ten years before they were an accepted commodity in many homes. In the 1970s and 1980s, it took five years to bring a new car from conception to manufacture – today the Japanese do this in less than twelve months. Consider the following tables:

Time	Mode of transport	Speed	Volume
6000 BC	Camel	8 mph	Low
1600 BC	Chariot	20 mph	Low
1784	Mail coach	10 mph	Low
1825	Steam train	13 mph	Medium
1885	Combustion engine	20 mph	High
1903	Airplane	50 mph	High
1960	Spaceship	18,000 mph	Low

Time	Communication method	Speed	Volume
6000 BC	Information by camel	8 mph	Low
1600 BC	Information by chariot	20 mph (max.)	Low
1784	Information by mail coach	10 mph	Low
1794	Telegraph	Seconds	Low
1876	The telephone	Conversational speed	Low
1942	Computers	Seconds	Low
1960	Networked computers	Seconds	Medium
1984	Silicon microchip	Nanoseconds	High

Figure 8.1

If you were to plot the changes from the two tables on a graph, they would both look like Figure 8.2.

Speed

6000 BC   1900

Time

Figure 8.2: Speed of communication; speed of transport; speed of change

**In the 1990s, lead-times for new products and services
are talked of in months not years.**

Reasons for shorter lead-times:

- Technology.
- The ability to communicate almost instantaneously.
- The ability to move goods quickly and freely between markets.
- Consumer pressure.
- An organization's need to grow.
- An organization's need to survive.

An organization is nothing more than a collection of human objectives, expectations and obligations. It performs through a structure of roles, both planned and unplanned in a proactive or reactive way. Its *aim* is to generate money – its *objective* is to make a financial surplus.

To manage these human interactions within an organization in a creative and dynamic way, and to compete in the fast-changing customer-orientated market, you need a *tool kit* of competent and reliable professional techniques which will enable you to take control, measure outcomes, and respond effectively.

The analysis, control and effective managing of all organizational issues can be dealt with by following the PANDA methodology of problem-solving.

**The greatest potential for control
tends to exist at the point where action takes place.**

The PANDA problem-solving discipline

Using the five-point discipline enables you systematically to remove failure from any given process. It is a disciplined series of steps which utilizes the dynamics of teamwork to achieve successful outcomes. There are five steps in the process:

1. *Prepare:* This process involves defining the problem and establishing the root cause(s) of the problem.
2. *Act:* This process involves generating solutions that will measure criteria and confirm the root cause(s).
3. *Navigate:* This process involves defining a planned route that will establish objectives and planned solutions.
4. *Do:* This process activates and implements the planned route (planned solutions) with appropriate measures and controls.
5. *Assess:* This process measures the positive actions and establishes the new process as the new standard.

P R E P A R E
A
N
D
A

Stage 1: Prepare
Defining the problem
To define the problem clearly is the most important issue in identifying an effective solution. It is essential that all the stakeholders involved in the problem are represented, and play an active role in verbalizing the definition. Remember, it is people who get things done. Successful problem-solving depends upon *ownership*. A person will not own an initiative unless they have been involved in its development.

Analyze for root cause(s)
The analysis of the problem must be structured and controlled. The choice and use of Consensus Analytical Tools and Techniques (CATT) are critical in

finding the root cause(s) of the problem. Without finding the root cause(s), any solutions implemented will only hide the problem and allow it to reoccur.

If you do not know why it is happening, you will not concentrate your efforts on the corrective action. If you think you know why it is happening and you are incorrect, then any action you take will be misguided and wrong.

It is not what you find – it is what you do about it!

P
A C T
N
D
A

Stage 2: Act
Generate solutions
Generating solutions needs to be done using as much objectivity as possible. Of course intuition and experience come into many decisions. The use of structured and participative tools and techniques ensures consistent results and ownership. During this phase, you need to define the measures to be used that will control and monitor your proposed solution(s).

P
A
N A V I G A T E
D
A

Stage 3: Navigate
Plan the route to the solution
After defining the problem, analyzing root causes and generating solutions, it is necessary to define a *plan* of action which will establish objectives and determine responsibilities for action.

P
A
N
D O
A

Stage 4: Do
Put measure(s) in place, implement and verify
Set up agreed measures, then implement them through the established and agreed PLAN. Through the measures set up, you can now clearly see the effect of the changes implemented, and if the change is working then you can go to the next stage at the appropriate time.

If, however, the change is not working, then you will have objective data to analyze and you can go back to:

Stage 1: to determine if you really found the root cause the first time;

or

Stage 2: what was it about your original solution that caused it to fail?

P
A
N
D
ASSESS

Stage 5: Assess
Standardize
You only get to this stage when all parties agree that the problem has truly been resolved. Then, and only then, are the procedures written down and/or changed.

**It is not the situation but your reaction to the situation
which determines success.**

There is a powerful kit of tools that complements the five-point problem-solving discipline. They are collectively known as the Consensus Analytical Tools and Techniques – CATTs. Figure 8.4 shows a matrix of when these different tools and techniques are used.

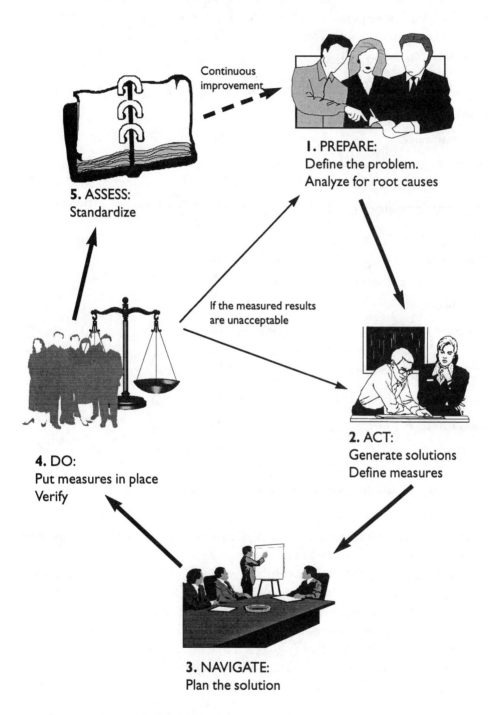

Continuous
improvement

1. PREPARE:
Define the problem.
Analyze for root causes

5. ASSESS:
Standardize

If the measured results
are unacceptable

2. ACT:
Generate solutions
Define measures

4. DO:
Put measures in place
Verify

3. NAVIGATE:
Plan the solution

Figure 8.3: The five-point problem-solving discipline diagram

The most important thing to remember is that all improvements, no matter how small or large, *must* contribute to the mission statement and objectives of the organization. Therefore everything you do *must* be focused on these two critical elements.

	Propose	Act	Navigate	Do	Assess
MUST HAVE:					
Mission statement	✓	✓	✓	✓	✓
Objectives	✓	✓	✓	✓	✓
TOOLS & TECHNIQUES:					
Team affinity brainstorming	✓	✓	✓		
Fishbone diagram	✓	✓	✓		
Critical success factor matrix	✓	✓	✓		
Check sheet			✓	✓	
Flow chart	✓	✓	✓	✓	
Force field analysis	✓	✓	✓		
Histogram	✓	✓	✓	✓	✓
Pareto analysis	✓	✓	✓	✓	
Steady state control chart		✓	✓	✓	✓
Spider diagram		✓	✓	✓	✓

Figure 8.4: Consensus Analytical Tools & Techniques Matrix (CATTs Matrix)

It is important to remember that in all cases it is *people* who make quality improvements, *not the quality tools.*

The following tools are powerful, structured and consistent techniques for measuring and recording, which should allow for all relevant issues of a problem to be addressed. It should, however, be noted that if the people involved do not have the necessary ability or knowledge to discuss the aspects involved, then the tools will not make up for these shortcomings.

These quality tools and techniques allow only intelligent and knowledgeable people to make consistent and informed decisions.

Organizational mission statements (OMS)

It is essential that before you attempt to solve any problem within an organization, you clearly understand the mission statement of that organization and you have it available in writing. *A mission statement is not the same as the organizational objectives.*

An organizational mission statement consists of two elements:

1. The vision of the organization.
2. The values or principles of the organization.

These two elements may be separate or integrated into one statement.

The vision
This is the ideal destination. It is where the organization wants to go.

The values
These are the beliefs behind any action by the organization.

Sometimes it can be difficult to distinguish between the two elements. For this reason, it is easier to brainstorm the two elements together in order to arrive at a meaningful OMS. A vision may be one statement, or a number of statements.

Vision is the gift of seeing clearly what may be.
Vision expands our horizons.
The more we see, the more we can achieve.
The courage to follow our dreams is the first step towards destiny.

See things and say 'Why?'
Dream things that never were and say 'Why not?'

Objectives

In order to manage effectively you need to know very clearly what you are trying to achieve. OMS 'Objectives' are statements derived from the organizational mission statement that define *how* the OMS will be achieved.

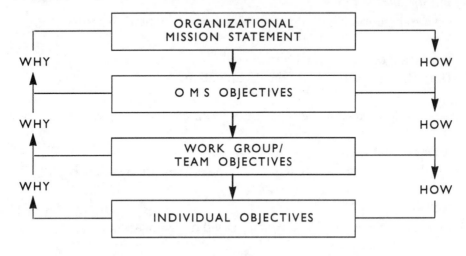

Figure 8.5

Work group or team objectives are derived from the OMS objectives, and individual objectives are derived from the work group or team objectives.

- The question WHY takes you up a level.
- The question HOW takes you down a level.

The number of levels would vary with the size and structure of the organization.

To help define the mission statement and objectives, you should use the TAB technique which I am about to describe.

High achievement always takes place within the framework of high expectations and dreams.

Team Affinity Brainstorming (TABS)

'Normal brainstorming' is a technique for generating ideas in a group. The members of the group meet and express ideas as they think of them. These ideas are written down on a flip chart or board. No one is allowed to comment or make judgements on any of the ideas at the time: the object being to compile a list for subsequent consideration and evaluation. This group participation tends to generate ownership for the final solution.

The 'Delphi technique' is similar to brainstorming, only each member or interested party submits his recommendations or views on the issue to a central contact point. All ideas generated in this way are then circulated to all those participating in the process, each of whom then has an opportunity to submit comments on them. This process is repeated until a consensus emerges. Although time-consuming, it can be an effective approach to the management of change and/or problem-solving, as it enables all parties to express their views. Thus it tends to generate ownership to the final outcome or solution.

TABS is a mixture of the above techniques, and I believe it is a more powerful proactive tool than either of them. It can be used for:

- creative thinking;
- collecting a large number of ideas;
- helping to eliminate chaos;
- identifying many causes, effects, solutions and possibilities relating to any given problem(s).

Facilitation
To use the following processes and gain the most from them, I believe that they should be conducted through an independent facilitator. An independent facilitator is someone who is skilled in guiding and leading teams through a structured process, but who may not necessarily be a stakeholder in the activity. Facilitation works best when the facilitator has no direct input into the content of the process, but simply conducts and ensures that the methodology and structured process is followed. This function is usually carried out by someone independent of the organization, or a member of the training department within the organization.

Over the next few pages I will explain the process involved in Team Affinity Brainstorming (TAB), then I will show the compilation of a fishbone diagram from the TAB analysis. I will then explain the construction and use of a 'critical success factor matrix'. After explaining these techniques, I will show the reader an actual working example of the whole process from start to finish.

This technique is very powerful and although it can be completed by an individual, it is more effective when it is done with a team in a controlled and structured way. Each step has been explained carefully. It does take time to implement and actually work through the technique *but* the rewards, if the process is done professionally, are significant.

How to carry out a Team Affinity Brainstorm session
The process has two distinct parts.

Part 1 of the process has three stages:

TAB 1.0 Stage A

- A *facilitiator* is required to manage and control the session.
- A quiet, comfortable room with blank walls is required.
- Packs of 'Post-It' notes are required.
- A flip chart and/or whiteboard is required.

TAB 1.1 Stage A

- Arrange all the interested parties together in the room. If possible, the participants should be seated in a circle or semi-circle with the facilitator in the middle, or they should be seated around a table with the facilitator at one end. It is important that all participants can see each other.
- The facilitator should state the problem and check to ensure everyone understands it. This stage is very important. Time must be spent on writing down, in a clear and unambiguous way, the problem or objective of the TABS, on a flip-chart or board so that everyone can see it. If the problem or objective has to be agreed by the team, then time should be spent on wordcrafting the statement for consensus agreement. The problem or objective must be clearly stated and agreed by everyone before moving to Stage 1.2

TAB 1.2 Stage A

- All team members must have a pen and a pad of 'Post-It' sticky notes.
- Each team member is invited to think of ideas that affect the problem or the objective and *to PRINT the idea on a 'Post-It' note BEFORE saying the idea aloud to the whole team.* When an individual has verbalized an idea he places the 'Post-It' note to one side and thinks of some more ideas.
- No one is allowed to question or make a judgement on any suggestion made. The process is one of building and developing, not questioning.
- It is important that everyone is involved and encouraged to verbalize as many ideas as possible – creativity and lateral thinking should be encouraged.

TAB 1.3 Stage A

The facilitator should motivate and actively push the team to verbalize as many ideas as possible. This process should not be limited to a time, but allowed to flow for as long as ideas are forthcoming from the team.

TAB 1.4 Stage A

When the facilitator feels the team have exhausted their thoughts he should then ask each member of the team for one last suggestion. The facilitator should ask each team member individually for his final idea, ensuring of course that it is PRINTED on the 'Post-It' note first.

TAB 1.5 Stage A

It is useful at this point to have a break of at least ten minutes to allow the participants to relax and regenerate their thoughts.

THIS ENDS TAB STAGE A

TAB 1.6 Stage B

- After the break the facilitator should ask each individual to stick his 'Post-It' notes on the blank walls.
- When all the 'Post-It' notes have been placed on the walls, then move to the next step.

TAB 1.7 Stage B

The following step should not be limited by constraints of time.
- *The team must decide when this stage is complete.*
- The purpose of this stage is to put ideas together for analysis by moving the 'Post-It' notes into groups.

TAB 1.8 Stage B

The rules are:

- *No one is allowed to talk.*
- A blank sheet of flipchart paper will be designated as the SinBin.
- Participants must walk around the room, looking at every single 'Post-It' note. They must then decide *for themselves* which ideas are linked.
- Individuals must take responsibility for moving 'Post-It' notes together into groups.
- It is usual for someone to move a note to one group and for someone else to then move the same note to another group. This process can continue until the team decide that the idea is in the right group. When quiet conflicts exist, it is acceptable for contentious ideas to be put into a separate group for further thought by the team. The facilitator will ensure that conflicts do not get out of hand, and will take the initiative. The SinBin is useful for this purpose and any 'Post-It' note moved on to the SinBin can not be touched for ten minutes. This usually resolves any conflict. Under no circumstances must any member of the team (including the facilitator) initiate rank over any other member in relation to the grouping of ideas. The purpose of completing this part of the technique in silence is to make every member think, not only about how he perceives the situation, but about how others perceive the situation.

TAB 1.9 Stage B

When the team is satisfied that all the related 'Post-It' notes have been grouped together, it is again advisable to have a break.

THIS ENDS TAB STAGE B

TAB 1.10 Stage C

- The facilitator should now gather the team members around each of the groups of 'Post-It' notes in turn and, through discussion, agree a HEAD-ING or TITLE for the group of ideas. It may be that one of the 'Post-It' notes makes an acceptable heading, or it may be that the facilitator has to print a heading onto a new 'Post-It' note. The heading or title should be short and meaningful.
- When this has been completed, the team should be thanked for their initial participation and allowed to leave.

THIS ENDS THE FIRST PART OF THE TABS PROCESS

Part two of the TAB process

The facilitator is responsible for the following activities.

TAB 2.1

- Each group of 'Post-It' notes, with their main heading, should be carefully placed in a large envelope. The heading/title of the group should be marked on the envelope as a reference.
- The facilitator should now retreat to a quiet office, preferably with a computer facility.

A fishbone diagram

Using the groups of 'Post-It' notes, compile a fishbone diagram (Figure 8.6). Use the heading or title of each group as the 'Bone' main heading on the diagram. Then write each of the associated ideas down the 'bone structure'. Write the problem or objective in the subject box.

The purpose of a fishbone diagram is to consolidate the TAB session and to communicate the results of the TAB session for further analysis.

Distribute a copy of the fishbone diagram to all the members of the team who participated in the Team Affinity Brainstorm session.

THIS ENDS THE TEAM AFFINITY BRAINSTORM PROCESS.

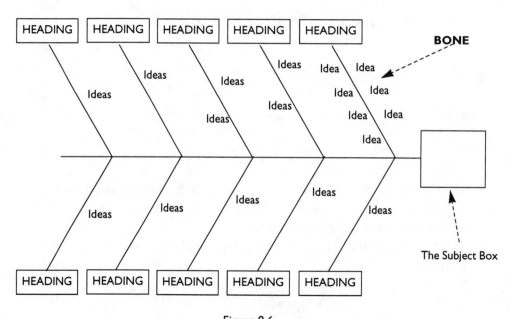

Figure 8.6

The next process is to prioritize the actions and activities identified, and allocate resources.

Critical success factors (CSF)

CSFs are used to determine the priority and importance of an activity, relative to the mission or objectives agreed. They identify what activity will impact the mission or objectives the greatest, and *why*. This will then allow management to allocate the necessary resources to the right activities.

To determine CSFs, you should measure against the organizational mission statements or the company objectives. If the CSFs that are to be determined come from a generic organizational problem, then you should measure against the mission statements. If the CSFs to be determined come from a department or divisional problem, then the company objectives could be used, but you could also use the mission statements.

To determine CSFs you need to construct a CSF *matrix*.

How to construct the CSF matrix
1. Write the mission statements or objectives into the columns A to G.
2. Write the activities to be assessed in the rows 1 to 8. You can obviously

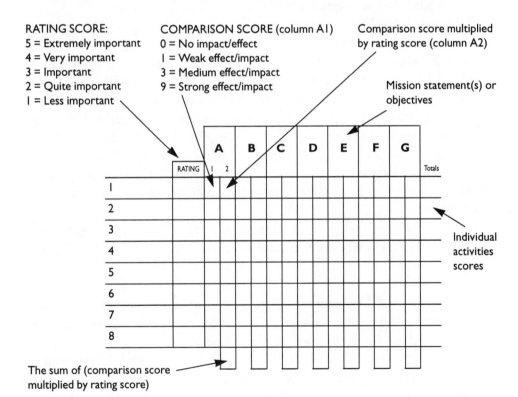

Figure 8.7: A critical success factor matrix

have many more activities than eight: list them all. These activities come from your TAB sessions and are the main headings from the fishbone diagram.

3. Setting the RATING level requires judgement, and needs the team to be in agreement. A team consensus must be reached in each case. This process needs a facilitator. Only use 5 as High Importance down to 1 as Low Importance. At no time does this imply that something on the list is not important – but the team have to decide what on the list of activities is more important than something else. You should try to get an even spread of priorities – do not make everything a 5, or everything a 3. For the CSF process to be really effective, it is important that open and frank discussion is encouraged at the rating stage.

4.. When you have completed steps 1 to 3, read the first activity and ask the following question: 'HOW MUCH DOES THIS ACTIVITY IMPACT ON THE STATEMENT IN COLUMN A?' At this stage you have only one of four decisions:

   9 means it has a significant impact;
   3 means it has an impact;
   1 means it has little impact;
   0 means it has no impact.

The team should discuss and agree. You cannot use any other score except 9-3-1 or 0. The team must use consensus to arrive at its decision, *not a majority.* This is the main reason why a facilitator must be used for this process to be effective. Write the relevant score into the *left hand corner* of box A1. Continue with activity 1 by asking the same question about column 'B' and so on, until all the mission statement(s)/objectives have been dealt with. Then proceed with activity 2 and repeat the whole process until all activities have been assessed against all mission statements or objectives.

5. When this part of the process is complete, you need to have a break. During the break, some of the team should complete the calculations as follows:

   • Multiply each Comparison Score by the Rating Score and enter the number in the right-hand column box using a *red pen* or different colour from that used to enter the Comparison Score.

   • When all boxes have been multiplied out, total the *red numbers* in each column vertically and horizontally. (Column A1 is multiplied by Rating Score and the result is entered in column A2 – repeat for all listed activities down column A – then do column B and other columns the same.)

- By using Pareto analysis you can now establish which 20 per cent of the activities will give you 80 per cent of the impact needed to achieve your mission. (See my discussion of Pareto analysis on page 119 for details.)

These results may not be the results expected in all cases. Some will be, but some activities, surprisingly, come out with higher scores than expected. At this point the team should discuss its findings and, through consensus, agree that the outcome is owned by the team. It is permissible with consensus, to reappraise some of the previous decisions made.

What you should do now is discuss the CSF list of activities and decide how your resources will be allocated.

There follows next a working example of a fictitious company using the TAB process and the consequent development of a fishbone diagram followed by the construction of a CSF matrix.

You will see from this example that the process is extremely powerful in its ability to communicate and identify priorities. The effort put into the processes is high, but the outcomes can have significant positive effects on the organization and its financial surplus.

The whole process of TAB, fishbone diagram and CSF matrix compilation should in all cases be undertaken with the aid and guidance of a *trained facilitator.*

An example of the processes in action

On any journey involving change, the first step is usually the hardest: you have to start somewhere and establish the direction. This comes down to many factors, most of which at this stage are subjective, emotional feelings and judgement. But, if they are discussed in an open and free-flowing forum, with all the stakeholders having an input, then the results can be a very powerful tool for change. This process creates the *vision* and *mission* of the organization.

Once the direction has been established, *all* other problems and opportunities can be objectively measured against the mission.

The following is an example of the results of a TAB session with company XYZ.

The mission statement of XYZ Company is to be SIMPLY THE BEST by:

- conforming to legal and moral obligations;
- motivating and empowering all employees;
- developing an effective Company Business System;
- training and developing all employees to their full potential;
- building knowledge of the market place and customer requirements;
- developing a rapid response to market opportunities;
- reducing waste and overheads.

This communicates an unambiguous statement, to all stakeholders, of the clear intentions of the organization.

**Only when you have established the mission can you
start thinking about company objectives.**

The Board of Directors then set one *main objective* for the company:

To sustain profitable growth.

The Board then presented to the Senior Management Team their mission with the organizational objective. The purpose of this was to get the Senior Management Team to *own* and *agree with* the mission of the company and the main objective, as seen by the Directors.

(If, during the discussions with the Senior Management Team, it is felt by all participants that amendments or changes should be made, then they should be made.)

In this instance, the Senior Management Team felt that it was essential that the company recognized the unacceptable proliferation in part numbers and new materials being designed into their products. Because of this, they added a further comment to the mission which was altered to read:

The mission statement of XYZ Company is to be SIMPLY THE BEST by:

- conforming to legal and moral obligations;
- motivating and empowering all employees;
- developing an effective Company Business System;
- training and developing all employees to their full potential;
- building knowledge of the market place and customer requirements;
- developing a rapid response to market opportunities;
- reducing waste and overheads;
- *optimizing materials.*

The Directors and the Senior Management Team then followed the TAB technique to develop a set of divisional objectives that would support the main company objective of *sustained profitable growth.*

The problem was stated as: *'How do we sustain profitable growth?'*

The following list is printed in the groupings identified after Part 2 of the TAB process was completed. The ideas were grouped under main headings. They are identified below in bold type.

Deliver winning products quickly
- understand the market;
- reduce time to market;
- introduce new products.

Be proactive in the selling process
- support sales in selling;
- reduce manufacturing price;
- reduce selling price;
- maximize manufacturing price;
- convince sales that customer should pay more.

Increase customer value of our product
- increase customer satisfaction;
- increase customer value of the products.

Reduce material costs
- reduce the material costs;
- improve development with suppliers.

Optimize overheads
- reduce overheads;
- better control of overheads;
- reduce waste fixed/variable.

Build credibility in the market
- be seen as world class producer;
- raise the company profile in the market place;
- improve confidence with customers;
- influence the market direction.

Increase process and direct labour efficiency
- reduce process costs (direct).

The main headings from this TAB session were then taken by the Senior Management as their team objectives to achieve the main company objective of 'Sustain Profitable Growth'. In other words, this was *how* they were going to achieve the main objective set by the Board.

The next problem stated was: '*How* do we achieve these management objectives?'

The Senior Management Team then convened a TAB session and they came up with the following ideas. Each idea was printed on a 'Post-It' note.

- accurate and timely information
- actively seek profitable product opportunities
- advise/inform the community of our requirements
- application of new technology
- be a responsible partner to the community
- benchmark against the competition
- better utilization of what we have got
- build supplier partnerships
- choose suppliers to support UK economy
- communicate company objectives when defined
- compatibility of information throughout the company
- conform to legal requirements
- conform to moral obligations to the environment

- continuous improvement of suppliers through assessment
- control of change
- create more ownership and involvement
- customer feedback
- design through concurrent engineering
- develop people in a consistent way
- develop the individual to his potential
- devise a system to establish training needs
- employ a mechanism to understand the market
- employ the right skills
- ensure employees are motivated
- ensure personal safety and security of individuals
- find out what the customer wants
- get serious about health and safety issues
- improve communications
- improve company briefings
- improve customer contact
- improve design and test
- improve manufacturing process
- improve the working environment
- improve time to market
- integrated business system including CAD/CAM
- involvement with the community
- keep the community informed
- know the current true selling price
- know the market price
- manufacture and supply product to specification
- match skills of employees to the work they are set
- new applications for our products
- offer discounts and incentives
- product enhancements
- product reliability
- product reliability testing
- provide a satisfactory working environment
- provide product design to meet customer needs
- provide product training
- provide some security of employment
- provide support to the community
- rapid assimilation of customer feedback
- rationalization

- recognize employees' responsibility to their families
- reduce lead-times
- reduce rework
- reduce throughput time
- review supplier database
- reward and recognition
- show and be seen to show concern for the environment
- show concern and provide support to all employees
- simplified systems
- SPC controls
- succession planning
- suggestion scheme
- support local education
- technical service and support
- training and development
- understand what the customer wants on price
- user friendly
- value engineering
- variety reduction in materials
- work with Sales to find new markets

After a break the Senior Team then took the headings from the mission statements and used those headings to group their list of TAB ideas (which were printed on 'Post-It' notes). They did this by asking themselves the question, 'How are we going to . . . ?'

Example: How are we going to get accurate and timely information?
Answer: **Develop an effective company business system.**

**It is essential that every action
MUST fit with the overall mission of the organization.**

The following is how the managers allocated each of the ideas generated in the HOW session under the Mission Statement headings:

Conform to legal and moral obligations
- provide a satisfactory working environment
- keep the community informed
- support local education
- be a responsible partner to the community
- provide support to the community

- involvement with the community
- choose suppliers to support UK economy
- conform to legal requirements
- ensure personal safety and security of individuals
- get serious about health and safety issues
- conform to moral obligations to the environment
- show and be seen to show concern for the environment

Motivate and empower all employees

- reward and recognition
- suggestion scheme
- create more ownership and involvement
- show concern and provide support to all employees
- provide some security of employment
- ensure employees are motivated
- improve communications
- communicate company objectives when defined
- recognize employees' responsibility to their families
- improve company briefings

Develop an effective company business system

- compatibility of information throughout the company
- better utilization of what we have got
- accurate and timely information
- integrated business system including CAD/CAM
- user friendly
- control of change
- improve communication
- simplified systems

Train and develop all employees to their full potential

- match skills of employees to the work they are set
- develop people in a consistent way
- develop the individual to their potential
- employ the right skills
- devise a system to establish training needs
- succession planning
- provide product training
- training and development

Build knowledge of the market place and customer requirements
- customer feedback
- technical service and support
- know the market price
- know the current true selling price
- employ a mechanism to understand the market
- understand what the customer wants on price
- improve customer contact
- actively seek profitable product opportunities
- benchmark against the competition
- find out what the customer wants
- work with Sales to find new markets

Develop a rapid response to market opportunities
- improve time to market
- product enhancements
- offer discounts and incentives
- reduce lead-times
- design through concurrent engineering
- provide product design to meet customer needs
- technical service and support
- application of new technology
- new applications for our products
- rapid assimilation of customer feedback

Reduce waste and overheads
- SPC controls
- reduce rework
- product reliability testing
- improve design and test
- improve manufacturing process
- manufacture and supply product to specification
- product reliability
- reduce throughput time

Optimize materials
- continuous improvement of suppliers through assessment
- build supplier partnerships
- review supplier database
- rationalization
- value engineering
- variety reduction in materials

It was now possible to draw up a fishbone diagram (Figure 8.8).

- provide a satisfactory working environment
- keep the community informed
- support local education
- be a responsible partner to the community
- provide support to the community
- involvement with the community
- choose suppliers to support UK economy
- conform to legal requirements
- ensure personal safety and security of individuals
- get serious about health & safety issues
- conform to moral obligations to the environment
- show and be seen to show concern for the environment

- reward and recognize
- suggestion scheme
- create more ownership and involvement
- show concern and provide support to all employees
- provide some security of employment
- ensure employees are motivated
- improve communications
- communicate company objectives when defined
- recognize employees' responsibility to their families
- improve company briefings

- compatibility of information throughout the company
- better utilization of what we have got
- accurate and timely information
- integrated business systems including CAD/CAM
- user friendly
- control of change
- improve communication
- simplified systems

- match skills of employees to the work they are set
- develop people in a consistent way
- develop the individual to their potential
- employ the right skills
- devise a system to establish training needs
- succession planning
- provide product training
- training and development

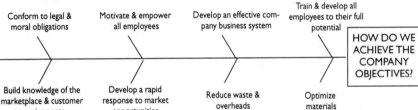

Conform to legal & moral obligations

Motivate & empower all employees

Develop an effective company business system

Train & develop all employees to their full potential

HOW DO WE ACHIEVE THE COMPANY OBJECTIVES?

Build knowledge of the marketplace & customer requirements

Develop a rapid response to market opportunities

Reduce waste & overheads

Optimize materials

- customer feedback
- technical service and support
- know the market price
- know the current true selling price
- employ a mechanism to understand the market
- understand what the customer wants on price
- improve customer contact
- actively seek profitable product opportunities
- benchmark against the competition
- find out what the customer wants
- work with sales to find new markets

- improve time to market
- product enhancements
- offer discounts and incentives
- reduce lead-times
- design through concurrent engineering
- provide product design to meet customer needs
- technical services and support
- application for new technology
- new applications for our product
- rapid assimilation of customer feedback

- SPC controls
- reduce rework
- produce reliability testing
- improve design and test
- improve manufacturing process
- manufacture and supply product to specification
- product reliablity
- reduce throughput time

- continuous improvement of suppliers through assessment
- build supplier partnerships
- review supplier database
- rationalization
- value engineering
- variety reduction in materials

COMPANY OBJECTIVES
- Develop winning products quickly
- Be proactive in the selling process
- Increase customer value of our project
- Reduce material costs
- Optimize overheads
- Build credibility in the market
- Increase process & direct labour efficiency

Figure 8.8: Fishbone diagram

The Team of Directors and Senior Managers now became one team, and they had to determine what action would have the greatest impact on the organization and thus determine what should be done first. They followed seven steps, as detailed below:

Step 1:

The facilitator drew up a critical success factor matrix for XYZ Company, showing the company mission statements across the top and the senior management objectives down the left axis (Figure 8.9).

			Company mission statements							
RATING SCORE: 5 = Extremely important 4 = Very important 3 = Important 2 = Quite important 1 = Less important		Conform to legal & moral obligations	Motivate & empower all employees	Develop an effective company business system	Train & develop all employees to their full potential	Build knowledge of the marketplace & customer requirements	Develop a rapid response to market opportunities	Reduce waste & overheads	Optimize materials	
Management Team Objectives	**Rating**									**Totals**
Deliver winning products quickly	5									
Be proactive in the selling process	2									
Increase customer value of our product	3									
Reduce material costs	5									
Optimize overheads	4									
Build credibility in the market	3									
Increase process & direct labour efficiency	3									

Figure 8.9

Step 2:
With the help of the facilitator, the Senior Management and Directors allocated a rating score to each of the senior management objectives, based on the key in the diagram. It must be noted that all objectives are classed as important – but some are assessed as more important than others. This rating score must be the consensus of the team, and not a majority decision. The facilitating role in this instance is extremely important.

Step 3:
When the rating score for each objective had been agreed, the facilitator took the first objective and asked the team to compare the effect of that objective, on each of the mission statements. This was done through consensus, not by a majority vote. There are only four possible scores:

0 = No effect
1 = Weak effect
3 = Medium effect
9 = Strong effect

The team *must* decide through consensus a score for each company mission statement in turn. Each team objective is then discussed in turn, and a score allocated accordingly.

Step 4:
When all the comparison scores had been completed, the facilitator multiplied the *rating score* by the *comparison score*. He then added the columns. (See Figure 8.10 & 8.11).

Step 5:
After the results had been seen, the whole team discussed the outcome to see if the calculated results were in line with common sense and practical possibilities.

In this case, everyone agreed that 'Developing a rapid response to market opportunities' was the first priority as it scored highest with 189 points. However the second highest 'Motivating & empowering employees' came before 'Train and develop all employees to their full potential'. Clearly, it would not make sense to motivate and empower employees until they had been trained. So, the team decided that 'Train and develop all employees to their full potential' would be second with 'Motivating & empowering employees' third.

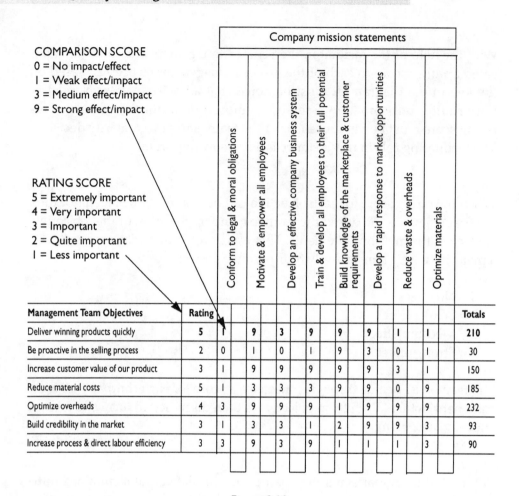

Figure 8.10

Step 6:
By looking at both sets of TAB results, it was now possible to determine *how* to proceed.

Example:
- 'Deliver winning products quickly' has an extremely important effect on 'Developing a rapid response to market opportunities'.
- To deliver winning products, the team have already agreed that they need to understand the market – reduce time to market and introduce new products and enhancements.
- To do this, they came up with a list of 'Hows' from a previous TAB session which were:

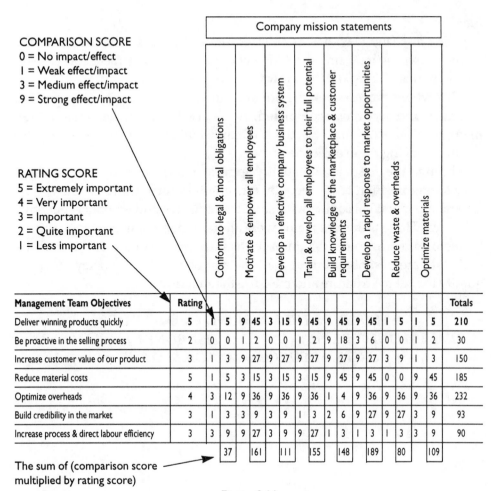

COMPARISON SCORE
0 = No impact/effect
1 = Weak effect/impact
3 = Medium effect/impact
9 = Strong effect/impact

RATING SCORE
5 = Extremely important
4 = Very important
3 = Important
2 = Quite important
1 = Less important

Company mission statements

Management Team Objectives	Rating	Conform to legal & moral obligations		Motivate & empower all employees		Develop an effective company business system		Train & develop all employees to their full potential		Build knowledge of the marketplace & customer requirements		Develop a rapid response to market opportunities		Reduce waste & overheads		Optimize materials		Totals
Deliver winning products quickly	5	1	5	9	45	3	15	9	45	9	45	9	45	1	5	1	5	210
Be proactive in the selling process	2	0	0	1	2	0	0	1	2	9	18	3	6	0	0	1	2	30
Increase customer value of our product	3	1	3	9	27	9	27	9	27	9	27	9	27	3	9	1	3	150
Reduce material costs	5	1	5	3	15	3	15	3	15	9	45	9	45	0	0	9	45	185
Optimize overheads	4	3	12	9	36	9	36	9	36	1	4	9	36	9	36	9	36	232
Build credibility in the market	3	1	3	3	9	3	9	1	3	2	6	9	27	9	27	3	9	93
Increase process & direct labour efficiency	3	3	9	9	27	3	9	9	27	1	3	1	3	1	3	3	9	90
		37		161		111		155		148		189		80		109		

The sum of (comparison score multiplied by rating score)

Figure 8.11

Develop a rapid response to market opportunities:
- improve time to market;
- product enhancements;
- offer discounts and incentives;
- reduce lead-times;
- design through concurrent engineering;
- provide product design to meet customer needs;
- technical service and support;
- application of new technology;
- new applications for our products;
- rapid assimilation of customer feedback.

Step 7:

A *project task force* was then established under the leadership of one of the team, to investigate, using the TAB technique again, the practicable day-to-day activities of *achieving* the 'Hows'.

This whole process took the organization XYZ Company some three to five days, and once it was completed, they had established the mission statement, the organizational objectives, the divisional objectives and the strategy for achieving these objectives.

Through the use of a total quality approach, this company was now in a very strong position to proceed, by forming task force teams that involved the stakeholders. This built ownership, commitment and workable, effective solutions. These task force teams were all trained in the use of team affinity brainstorming, fishbone diagrams, critical success matrix analysis and the tools that are described throughout the rest of the chapter. They used the quality toolkit to structure and measure their changes.

THIS ENDS THE WORKING EXAMPLE OF
TEAM AFFINITY BRAINSTORMING, FISHBONE DIAGRAM AND
CRITICAL SUCCESS FACTOR MATRIX.

Check sheet

The aim of a check sheet is to record the number of times that certain events happen, over a specific period of time, at a specific time frequency.

The method
- You specify a range of possible outcomes or events – it is recommended that you should not specify more than six to ten events, as it becomes more complex the more events you monitor.
- The people using the check sheet must understand the codes or meanings of the events listed.
- The unit of measurement must be specified – this could be the number of occurrences, or hours or costs.
- The frequency of monitoring must be established – hourly, daily, weekly.
- A check sheet blank must be produced. It is a practical idea to involve the people who will be collecting the data to help design the check sheet: this invokes ownership and clarifies the use of the form at the very beginning of the process.
- When presenting the findings and results, use Pareto or histograms to represent the data.

EVENTS	Mon	Tue	Wed	Thur	Fri	Mon	Tue	Wed	Thur	Fri	Totals
Unloading transport	\\\	✻	✻	✻	✻	✻	✻	✻	✻	✻	48
Loading transport		\\\				\\\			\\\	\\	11
Unpacking	\\\	✻\\	✻\\	✻	✻\\	✻	✻	✻		✻	50
Checking		✻			\\ ✻				✻		17
Administration	\\	\\\			\\	✻		\\		✻	19
Locating in shelf		\\\	✻		\\	\\	✻		\\		19
Issuing to assembly	\\\			\\	✻			✻	✻		20
Driving forklift truck	\\	✻	\\	✻	✻	✻	✻	✻	✻	✻	44
General duties	\\\	\\						✻			10
Miscellaneous	\\	\\		\\		\\\					9

Figure 8.12: Check sheet for analyzing articles in stores over a two-week period

Some uses of a check sheet

A check sheet has many uses:

- It could be used to record the number of times your telephone rings, or the number of times you are disturbed during a specific time of day. This analysis could then be used to reschedule your routine, or justify a secretary, or reallocate resources.
- It could be used to record any repetitive activity over a specific period of time for further analysis.
- It could be used as a check list to ensure that specific actions are taken or certain activities are undertaken. For example every time a component is placed in the outer carton you would mark the component box on the check sheet. This would show how many of which components were used in a particular time period.
- It can be used as a team activity measure. The names of all team members are listed as the events, and every time a team member contributes to the meeting they are given a mark. This analysis can show who is contributing the most or the least to a meeting. Of course, quantity does not mean quality and this analysis may not indicate anything on its own. However with other criteria linked to interpersonal skills, it could show when people are interrupting or disrupting the meeting.

You should be creative and innovative when using check sheets as they can be a quick and effective means of gathering varied data and information.

NAME	Interrupts	Summarizes	Builds on ideas	Questions and seeks clarification	Argues	COMMENTS

Figure 8.13: Meeting check sheet

Flow charts

The aim of a flow chart is to communicate a sequence of processes identifying key decision points, inputs and outputs.

The method
- Identify all the activities in the process or problem being investigated. It is useful to use 'Post-It' notes for this action. When writing on the 'Post-It' note, you should identify whether it is an input, an output, a decision or part of the process. This will help to clarify your thoughts and assist in drawing a detailed flow chart later.
- Put the list of activities into sequence by moving the 'Post-It' notes around on a board or blank wall.
- Work through the sequence on the 'Post-It' notes, identifying all the inputs, decisions and connections.
- When the sequence of activities looks correct, you should draw the flow chart.

There is a simplified version of a flow chart that uses only 'blocks', and there are more detailed flow charts that use different symbols to represent specific activities.

The following example will use both a block flow chart and a detailed flow chart to illustrate their respective uses.

A block flow chart
For the purpose of this example I will use the process of boiling an egg on a gas hob. To show the processes involved in boiling an egg I must first write down the activities (individual processes) involved:

- Select appropriate pan and fill with sufficient water to cover an egg.
- Place pan on to the gas hob, and carefully light the hob.
- Bring water to the boil.
- Select egg.
- Select an appropriately sized spoon to place egg into boiling water.
- Carefully place egg into boiling water, using spoon.
- Measure the time the egg is in the boiling water to equate to the type of egg required:
    Five minutes for a hard boiled egg;
    Three minutes for a soft boiled egg.
    Note: the time may vary depending on the size of the egg.

- When time has elapsed, turn off the gas hob and place the pan on a flat heat-resistant surface.
- Carefully remove the egg with the spoon.
- Place the egg in an eggcup and serve.
- Dispose of hot water from the pan.

I will now draw a simple block flow chart to represent the process described above (Figure 8.14).

It can be seen that the block flow chart communicates the processes more clearly than the list of written instructions, and conveys the message to the reader that specific processes have to be done before others. It shows which processes have direct influences on others, and which are independent.

The block flow chart can be enhanced by using lines with arrow heads, and the blocks could be numbered. Notice how, in some blocks, the reader is referred to other instructions. These are general instructions which have to be followed many times by different processes. In this particular case, every time a pan is removed from the gas hob it should be placed on a heat resistant surface. There will be specific health and safety procedures which will need to be followed. This specific process could have its own block flow chart. The same principle applies to the time chart instruction. There will be different time requirement for different sizes of egg and different types of boiled egg (hard or soft boiled).

Uses of block flow charts
- When there is not sufficient information to create a detailed flow chart.
- When you need to clarify and communicate a process quickly.
- To enhance and explain someone's job description.
- As a thinking tool to clarify your thoughts.
- As a reminder to do specific activities in a specific sequence.
- As a time management tool.
- As a chronological list of when events happened, and the relationships and consequences of those events.

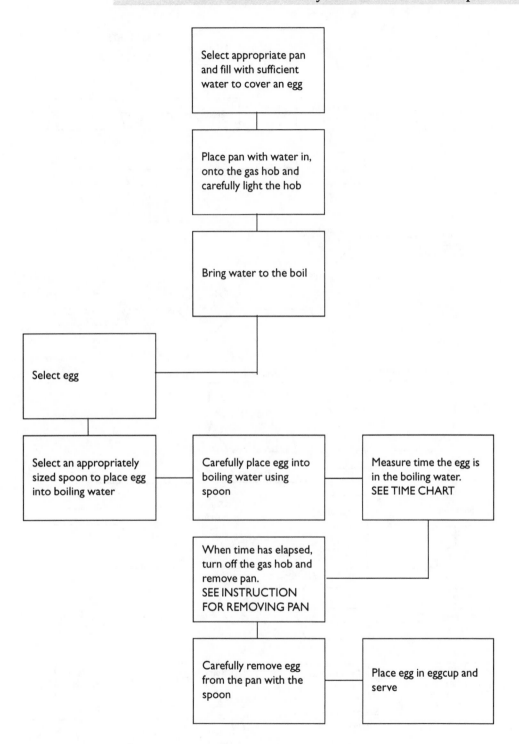

Figure 8.14: Block flow chart showing the simple process of boiling an egg

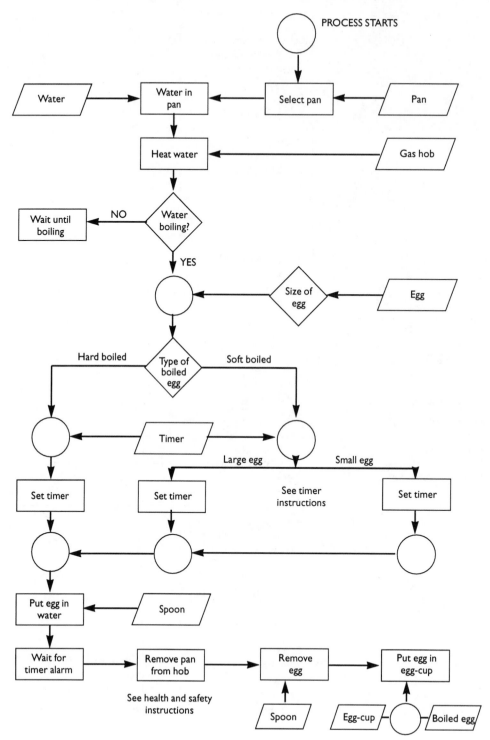

Figure 8.15: A detailed flow chart

A detailed flow chart
This type of flow chart uses different symbols to represent different types of activities:

| Input or output | Process | Decision | Connector |

Detailed flow charts are very useful, for the same reason I gave in relation to block flow charts – the difference being that they can express a great deal more information.

The detailed flow chart differentiates inputs and decisions from processes, helping to clarify and communicate more effectively.

When solving problems, this quality tool is extremely useful if it is designed with 'Post-It' notes, as they can be moved around to allow ideas and suggestions to be discussed in a dynamic and active way. Additions, amendments and deletions can quickly be incorporated and the activity can involve the whole team in an interactive way much more effectively than a static diagram on a piece of paper.

Once the process flow or problem flow has been agreed, then the flow chart can be drawn up on to a piece of paper for distribution, recording, or reporting purposes.

Force field analysis

The aim of a force field analysis is to identify the key forces for and against change, so that positive elements can be developed and negative elements can be contained, reduced or eliminated.

Method
- Identify all the stakeholders who are interested and/or involved in the process being addressed.
- Involve representatives from all the stakeholders in Part One of a Team Affinity Brainstorm session to:
  a) identify all the positive forces for change (*driving forces*).
  b) identify all the negative forces for change (*restraining forces*).
- Draw these forces of change in a diagram form that shows the positive forces pushing against the negative forces (see examples below).
- Identify those forces that are internal to the organization and mark them with an (I)
- Identify those forces that are external to the organization and mark them with an (E)
- Discuss the *driving* and *restraining* forces with the team and develop a strategy for moving forward.

It is essential, for an effective outcome, that all the stakeholders are reliably represented in the identification and discussion of the force field. It is important to record all forces, no matter how insignificant they may first appear. Remember that no personal judgement should be made when a stakeholder suggests a (driving or restraining) force. The development of a force field analysis is very much a subjective situation.

How to draw a force field

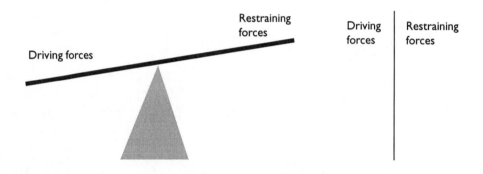

There follows an example of a force field for proposed changes required to introduce a quality approach into an organization.

DRIVING FORCES:
Promise of greater rewards (E)
Threats (E and I)
Wish for better image (E and I)
Customer complaints (E)
Desire to do better (I)
Pressure from shareholders (E)
Pressure from stakeholders (E and I)

RESTRAINING FORCES:
Lack of knowledge about problems (I)
Short staffed (I)
Low morale (I)
Poor equipment (I)
Late output (I)
Poor quality (I)
'Nothing in it for us' (I)

Criteria for change

- Every situation has forces driving it towards change, as well as forces restraining it from changing.
- In order to make the change, the driving forces have to be stronger than the restraining forces.
- This can be done by augmenting the driving forces, or reducing the restraining forces.
- The list of driving and restraining forces will be different, depending on who is doing the analysis.
- The driving forces consist of pressures to change and assets which will help to bring about change.
- Most of the restraining forces are the attitudes of the people.
- These attitudes have to be understood and altered if the change is to be implemented with commitment.
- The most sensible first step when planning change is to list all of the forces both driving and restraining, actual and potential.

You can enhance the diagram by underlining those issues which are thought to be more important or problematic. The thicker the line, the more important the problem is in the opinion of the team or individual drawing the force field.

The histogram

The aim of a histogram is to show the variability within a process over a period of time.

The method
- Gather statistical data relevant to the process being investigated.
- Determine the values to be used and sort the data accordingly.
- Plot the histogram.

You can draw histograms for many differing data issues. For example, we could draw a histogram to represent the analysis we carried out on the stores using the check sheet.

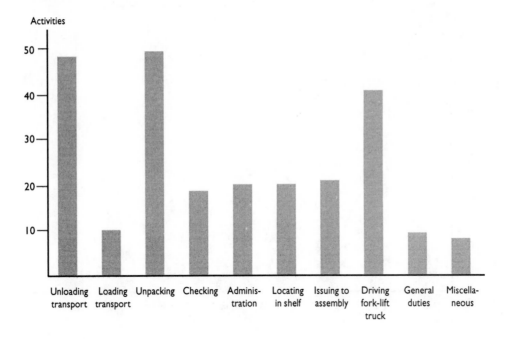

Figure 8.16

The histogram in Figure 8.16 clearly communicates that unpacking, unloading, and driving fork-lift trucks are the most frequent elements within the stores operation at this moment. Further analysis could now be done to see if these activities are being carried out effectively or resourced efficiently.

A histogram could be drawn for sets of data showing the age of the employees working in a particular organization (Figure 8.17).

AGE BAND	NUMBER OF EMPLOYEES
17 to 21	10
22 to 25	8
26 to 30	15
31 to 45	20
46 to 50	15
51 to 55	20
56 to 60	10
Over 60	5
Total employees	103

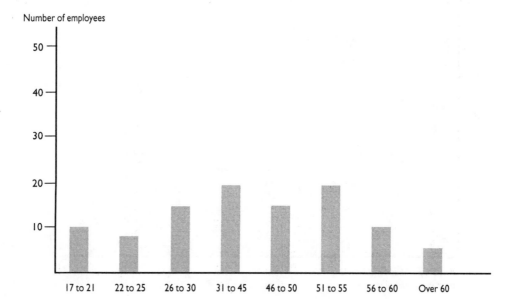

Figure 8.17

This data could then be shown to the senior managers of the organization, who would need to plan for five retirements in the next few years as well as possible replacements or job changes.

When thinking of making certain changes, it may be necessary to consider the age and gender mix within the organization, as this may help in deciding how to plan and implement new training.

Pareto analysis

The aim of Pareto analysis is to prioritize those areas in a process or situation which will give the most benefit with the least resources.

Pareto analysis aims to help you identify which problem areas should be tackled first in order to gain the maximum benefit for minimum effort, cost, or whatever other factor is involved. Its importance lies in the 80/20 rule that Pareto derived: namely, that in common experience, the vast majority of problems can be attributed to a small minority of causes.

To identify if the 80/20 rule applies, you need to analyze and rank the data according to a single factor. To do this, you must identify the factor you are using for comparison. It could be for example, cost, space or time.

The method
• Use check sheets or data lists to collect data.
• Rank data in the order that is relevant to the problem being addressed.
• Calculate 80 per cent of the element being investigated.
• Plot the ranked data using a histogram.

A working example of Pareto analysis
The following data in Figure 8.18 was made available from the stores depart-ment regarding items in stock. You have to calculate, using Pareto analysis, which part numbers represent 80 per cent of the value of inventory held in stock.

- Step 1: In Figure 8.18 below, complete the blank columns.
- Step 2: Then, in Figure 8.19, enter the details of each part number in descending order of total cost value. In other words, list the inventory by the greatest value first followed by the next greatest value.
- Step 3: Calculate 80 per cent of the grand total value of inventory and then establish how many and which items reflect that value, by referring to Figure 8.19.
- Step 4: Plot the values of each item from Figure 8.19 on a histogram in descending order of inventory value, and draw a vertical line identifying 80 per cent of the total value. The part number of each item should be along the 'x' axis (bottom horizontal line) – the 'y' axis should show value in £000s.

You can now plot a dotted line, indicating 80 per cent of the total value of inventory. From this, you can determine the number of items that affect 80 per cent of the value of the inventory – therefore by concentrating tighter control on these items only, you can control 80 per cent of your inventory costs. If you want to reduce your inventory, then concentration on these top items will yield greater benefit in a shorter space of time with limited resource. (Figure 8.21).

Note: where there are two part numbers which have the same total stock value (part number 1234 and part number 1237), you should always rank the part number with the highest unit value first. The reason for this is that the implication of losing one of the part numbers with the higher unit value, has a greater bearing on the financial surplus of the organization.

Typically, if this exercise were carried out in an average organization with 3,000 part numbers in stock, the analysis would indicate, that approximate-ly 500–600 part numbers would represent 80 per cent of the total value of the inventory. Controlling 500–600 part numbers tightly will use less resources in time and people than controlling the whole 3,000. It will also give control to 80 per cent of the organization's inventory assets.

Part number	Quantity	Unit cost £	Total cost (B x C)	Cumulative cost
A	B	C	D	E
1234	1000	1.00		
1235	34	200.00		
1236	133	5.00		
1237	100	10.00		
1238	85	60.00		
1239	77	45.00		
1240	2	343.00		
1241	1	713.00		
1242	2000	0.35		
1243	1000	0.20		
GRAND TOTAL VALUE OF INVENTORY (G)				

Figure 8.18

Part number	Quantity	Unit cost £	Total cost (B x C)	Cumulative cost	% of grand total value
A	B	C	D	E	F
GRAND TOTAL VALUE OF INVENTORY (G)					

Figure 8.19

Part number	Quantity	Unit cost £	Total cost (B x C)	Cumulative cost
A	B	C	D	E
1234	1000	1.00	1000	1000
1235	34	200.00	6800	7800
1236	133	5.00	665	8465
1237	100	10.00	1000	9465
1238	85	60.00	5100	14565
1239	77	45.00	3465	18030
1240	2	343.00	686	18716
1241	1	713.00	713	19429
1242	2000	0.35	700	20129
1243	1000	0.20	200	20329
GRAND TOTAL VALUE OF INVENTORY (G)				20329

Part number	Quantity	Unit cost £	Total cost (B x C)	Cumulative cost	% of grand total value
A	B	C	D	E	F
1235	34	200.00	6800	6800	33%
1238	85	60.00	5100	11900	58%
1239	77	45.00	3465	15365	76%
1237	100	10.00	1000	16365	80%
1234	1000	1.00	1000	17365	85%
1241	1	713.00	713	18078	89%
1242	2000	0.35	700	18778	92%
1240	2	343	686	19464	96%
1236	133	5.00	665	20129	99%
1243	1000	0.20	200	20329	100%
GRAND TOTAL VALUE OF INVENTORY (G)				20329	

Figure 8.20: Answers to exercise on Pareto analysis

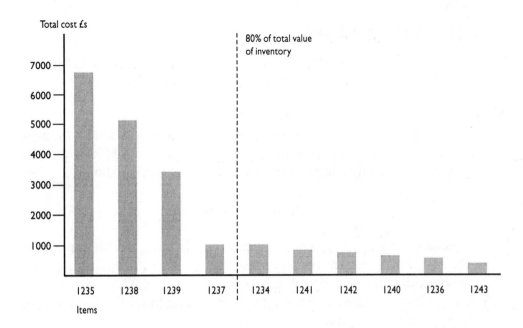

Figure 8.21: Bar chart of total costs

You can use Pareto in many different situations to prioritize and to get quick results from limited resources by separating the vital few from the trivial many. You need to use your imagination and be creative with this powerful tool.

Steady state control diagram

The aim of a steady state control diagram is to predict a process in order to reduce the variability of the output and eliminate defects.

The method
This is similar to statistical process control (SPC) but it does not involve the need for complicated statistical analysis. Steady state control (SSC) allows a process to be controlled without the need for complex calculations.

- Define the process that you wish to control.
- Identify the critical outputs.
- Determine the measurement frequency (hourly, daily, weekly, monthly).
- Determine the maximum acceptable upper and lower limits of the process, and plot these on a graph.
- Determine the control upper limit and the control lower limit – plot these lines on the same graph.
- Run the process and plot the measurements in the agreed frequency time limits.

Conformance provides the measure by which steady state management is judged a success or a failure. Managing for conformance can be seen as maintaining a balance between achieving certain output objectives and utilizing input resources.

In Figure 8.22, the upper and lower limits of the process have been plotted with a thin solid line. This means that if the process measurement goes above or below these limits, the process has produced scrap or errors.

The diagram also shows two thicker dotted lines. These are the control limits (upper and lower) and they define when action should be taken, either to stop errors being produced by the process or to ensure that the process continues to function. Any output from the process which is within the thin solid lines is acceptable to the customer and will satisfy requirements. (This could be an internal customer as well as an external customer.) A measurement on or outside the thick dotted lines and within the thin solid lines indicates that the process is going out of control, and action needs to be taken immediately.

Action should always be taken before waste is produced – not after.

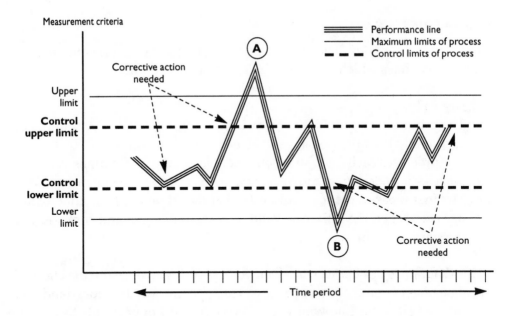

Figure 8.22: Steady state control chart (waste has been produced at points A and B)

You draw the X axis and mark off the time periods over which you wish to measure your process. These could be hours, days or weeks. The shorter the time period you measure the tighter the control. The decision on the length of the time period will be determined by how much confidence there is in the process staying within the acceptable limits set.

The Y axis is marked off with the measurement criteria. The upper and lower limits may be a dimension on a component, or they may be the number of absentees in a department. Taking the latter as a measure, the time periods could be in days and the measurement criteria could be the number of people absent. If the number of people not turning up for work exceeds the maximum limit you have set, then labour will need to be transferred into the department, or overtime will need to be worked to keep the department process going. If the number of people not turning up is very low and does not reach the lower limit, then this means that labour could be transferred to another department if required or overtime could be cut or reduced.

Steady state control charts can be used for many activities: they are only limited by your imagination. The power of the tool is in the fact that control and measurement is with the person doing the job – he can be empowered to take action when limits are reached.

Spider diagram

The aim of the spider diagram is to plot various related criteria and to measure the changes which occur over an agreed period of time.

The method
- The processes or activities to be measured must be related or connected, and should be expressed in general terms.
- The processes each form an independent leg of the spider diagram.
- Each leg is joined up to form a 'shape' of the processes being measured.
- The first measurements would establish the situation, then after action has been taken the activities could be measured again and compared to the starting position.

This diagram is very powerful when you are trying to measure the effect of change on an organization or process. The quickest way to understand this tool is to use it, so the following exercise gives you the opportunity to do that.

A working example of a spider diagram
The most important factor affecting anyone who wishes to improve his working life is *attitude*: the second most important factor is *the management of time*.

A major part of successful living lies in the ability to put first things first. Indeed, the reason why most major goals are not achieved is that we spend our time doing second things first. We need some means of how to value time, so that we can ensure the essentials are done, thus getting the greatest possible results from the least effort expended: a Pareto analysis of time.

Complete the exercise below by marking with a cross your score for each question on the matrix. Then write the number you have scored for each question in the column marked 'TOTAL'.

Be truthful.

Read each question and decide how well the question describes *you*. Do not answer the question in the way that you would *want* to be seen or the way that you think you should be seen – but in the way that you actually are now.

QUESTION 1:

I am ALWAYS in control of the way I spend my time.

Strongly agree				Agree				Strongly disagree	
9	8	7	6	5	4	3	2	1	TOTAL

QUESTION 2:

I NEVER feel rushed or obliged to do things I do not want to do.

Strongly agree				Agree				Strongly disagree	
9	8	7	6	5	4	3	2	1	TOTAL

QUESTION 3:

I NEARLY ALWAYS feel a sense of accomplishment from all my work.

Strongly agree				Agree				Strongly disagree	
9	8	7	6	5	4	3	2	1	TOTAL

QUESTION 4:

I DO NOT work long hours.

Strongly agree				Agree				Strongly disagree	
9	8	7	6	5	4	3	2	1	TOTAL

QUESTION 5:

I DO NOT take work home.

Strongly agree				Agree				Strongly disagree	
9	8	7	6	5	4	3	2	1	TOTAL

QUESTION 6:

My work does NOT make me feel stressed.

Strongly agree				Agree				Strongly disagree	
9	8	7	6	5	4	3	2	1	TOTAL

QUESTION 7:

I NEVER feel guilty about being unable to do a better job.

Strongly agree				Agree				Strongly disagree	
9	8	7	6	5	4	3	2	I	TOTAL

QUESTION 8:

I REALLY enjoy what I do.

Strongly agree				Agree				Strongly disagree	
9	8	7	6	5	4	3	2	I	TOTAL

QUESTION 9:

I can OFTEN find time to do things when I need.

Strongly agree				Agree				Strongly disagree	
9	8	7	6	5	4	3	2	I	TOTAL

QUESTION 10:

I take REGULAR and EFFECTIVE exercise.

Strongly agree				Agree				Strongly disagree	
9	8	7	6	5	4	3	2	I	TOTAL

QUESTION 11:

I plan and take REGULAR holidays and breaks.

Strongly agree				Agree				Strongly disagree	
9	8	7	6	5	4	3	2	I	TOTAL

QUESTION 12:

I NEVER put off doing difficult or boring work.

Strongly agree				Agree				Strongly disagree	
9	8	7	6	5	4	3	2	I	TOTAL

Plot the numbers from the column 'TOTAL' into the spider diagram below, and join the plots to make a shape of your time management. You now have hard evidence of your performance at the moment. If you measure yourself every month and over-draw your new measures on the spider diagram (perhaps using a different coloured pen) you will be able to see if and where you are improving. You should always be honest and truthful – you are only fooling yourself if you are not.

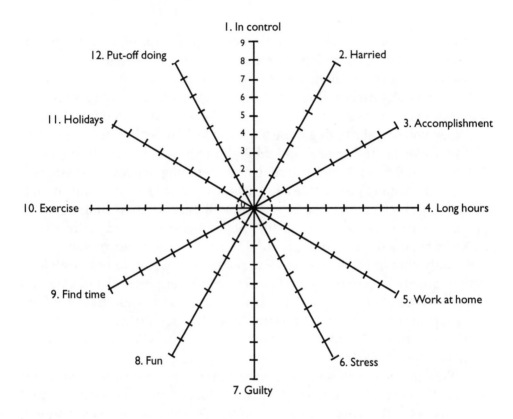

Figure 8.23: Time management spider diagram

The spider diagram is often used to summarize questionnaires, or any objective data that has been collected using a judgement scale. It is a very powerful communication tool, as the 'shape' drawn can easily be understood and improvements can be readily seen.

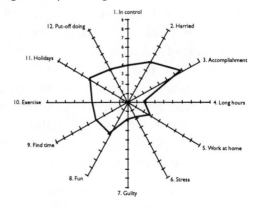

CHAPTER 9

A Summary of Part Two

Using 'quality tools' is like using any other process. If the input from the participants is not quality, then the fact that the process is a quality tool or technique will not make up for this. However, using quality tools and techniques will improve any process through the application of structured and consistent methodology. This will then be reflected in the output and feedback.

When you first start using these tools and techniques it is very important that you take the time to plan and think through what you are trying to do. The more time you put into planning and preparing, the less time you will waste and the more productive and effective you will be. The more you use the tools and techniques, the better you will become at creating new and powerful measures and controls which will result in improved performance.

Make the use of these tools a natural habit – an automatic routine.

Quality should be as instinctive as possible: you should not hesitate to deliver quality in everything you do. The customer (internal and external) can sense your reluctance when you hesitate or delay. Do not shy away from what appears to be a difficult problem. Tackle it using quality tools and techniques in a structured and consistent manner. You will surprise yourself with the depth of the creative solutions you develop.

Although most of these tools and techniques are meant for teams and groups, they can all be deployed by individuals – even the Team Affinity Brainstorm (TAB) technique. I often use the TAB technique when planning lectures, talks or client problems to help me understand the issues and develop strategies. This book was conceived and planned using the technique.

One of the most important things to remember while using the tools and techniques is to have *FUN*. Make the learning process enjoyable – get as many people as possible to participate. This way, the difficulties are shared and the learning process is strengthened.

The proliferation of discussion groups in many British companies today is testament to the powerful nature of participation. The following extract from the book, *Achieving Quality Performance*,[1] from a study of Land Rover shows what an impact such groups can have:

The managing directors of Land Rover Vehicles and Powertrain respectively clearly demonstrate their support by reading every set of minutes produced by the groups on site. They often comment personally on a problem, and make the effort to see as many groups as possible in action. On a practical level, it is through the managing directors' encouragement that their managers continue supporting the groups.

As the number of discussion groups has grown, the agendas of the mature groups have moved away from the working environment to concentrate on quality of product and process improvement. Discussion groups frequently report their successes to Rover board members at the quarterly business unit reviews, and an annual event is held to recognize all the groups' efforts. It has taken a lot of hard work and dedication, but the results are now speaking for themselves: over 500 problems were resolved in 1992.

The absolute importance of consistent communication throughout the levels of any organization cannot be stressed enough.

There is always more than one way to solve any problem. Solutions depend upon many varied influences, some of which we can never anticipate until they happen. No amount of planning can guarantee perfection or success – all we can ever hope to do is minimize the risks and give ourselves the best chance of achieving positive results.

**If failure was not an issue
what would you plan to do?**

Notes to Chapter 9
1. *Achieving Quality Performance*, edited by Richard Teare, Cyril Atkinson and Clive Westwood. London: Cassell, 1994; p. 122.

Part Three

CHAPTER 10

Quality Approach Case Studies

AIMS AND OBJECTIVES OF THIS CHAPTER

- To highlight actual cases of a quality approach in action.
- To provoke thought and encourage positive action.
- To support the ethos of a quality approach to work.

The following story was the original idea of Bill Harris-Heffer who works for the Royal Mail. The story is told in a simple narrative, and was written to be used as a means to demonstrate the basic concepts of a quality approach, to non-managerial staff.

The student and the lady

'Excuse me, I'm looking for the General Manager,' said a young student.

'Oh, you've come through the wrong door,' said the lady sweeping the floor. 'Who sent you this way?'

'Well, I looked at the directions that someone in the training group had sent me – but I think I've got a little lost.'

'Ah, the training group,' mused the lady; 'are you on a course or something?'

'No, not a course,' said the young student, 'I've come for an interview with the General Manager. I'm doing a business studies project at college and I need to understand how the business manages itself.'

'Well, that's interesting; in fact, you could not have come at a more exciting time.'

'Why, what's so exciting about *now*?'

The lady continued sweeping the floor. '*Now* is always exciting! In fact, *now* is all we can deal with. You see, we can learn from the past and plan for the future but *now* is what we must concern ourselves with immediately.'

The young man looked thoughtful. 'That's a bit shortsighted – I mean – well —' He fumbled for words and shuffled nervously on his feet.

'I thought the Royal Mail had been in business for over 350 years?'

'Yes, that's correct.' She continued to sweep the floor and empty the waste bin. 'But as I have just said, the past is no guarantee for the future. If we wish to stay in business for the next 350 years we must behave in the way that our customers expect us to behave *now*.'

The young student smiled and nodded. 'Yes, yes I can see what you mean.' He sat down on a chair next to a small table. He watched as she polished the furniture and dusted the telephone. 'But tell me, how does that fit into the way a business is managed? I mean, surely a business cannot just be managed in the present – it must plan for the future?'

She stopped cleaning and looked at the young man. 'Well, no business has a crystal ball – no business can actually see the future, so planning for something that you cannot know is going to happen is full of problems. However, you are partly correct – you see to plan for the future, you must manage today.'

'Yes, but what about investing for growth and higher profits?'

'That is done by managing today and looking at how we operate, how our competitors operate, what's happening with technology and listening to our customers, today.'

The young man reached inside his jacket for a pen and his notepad. 'It sounds quite complex, how is that actually done?'

She placed her sweeping brush against the wall and started to rearrange the magazines and papers on the small table in front of him. 'By a process called benchmarking. It means that we look at what other organizations are doing: not necessarily organizations in the same business as we are, just organizations who are doing things exceptionally well. We then look at what we are doing and see if we can improve our processes in similar ways.'

'Benchmarking – so it is like copying from others?'

She stopped rearranging the magazines and looked at him thoughtfully. 'No, not copying. Benchmarking is a method of assessing good practices which we then look at, in terms of our business, to see if we can either adopt the same principles or use the ideas to generate a better way for us to operate. It is a matter of learning from others – building and sharing ideas. You will find that what works in one business seldom works in another in exactly the same way. Ideas have to be shaped to fit the culture and working ethics of an organization.'

'How do you do that?'

'We use all of our employees. We tell them about the good idea and we investigate the possibility of the idea working in our business.'

'You mean that you ask the people on the shop floor and in the offices?'

'Yes.'

'But how will they know – or how can they possibly tell if the idea will work or not? What if it's a technical matter or something that they have never heard of?'

'All of our employees have been trained in the use of a problem-solving technique called PANDA, and the primary Consensus Analytical Tools and Techniques, which are quality tools.'

'What!'

She smiled. 'These are tools which allow cross-boundary teams of people to resolve any sort of problem in a structured and consistent way.'

'What's "cross-boundary"?'

'Well, cross-boundary teams are teams that are made up of people from different departments or functions.'

'So a department can get involved in another department's problems?'

'Absolutely,' she said, 'that ensures everyone owns the problems of the business and that any problem for one department is a problem for everyone in the organization.'

The student did not look up but he kept writing in his note book. 'But tell me, how does the organization know what ideas to look for and what ideas to ignore?'

'To start with, the organization has a mission statement and a set of objectives which have been set by the senior executives of the Royal Mail. These are used to develop a business plan. This business plan is communicated to every employee so that everyone knows what the business is trying to do and where it is trying to go. Every idea that comes along is reviewed in line with the business plan, and if it complements or adds value to the business plan then it is investigated and, if possible, implemented.'

'So the business plan is like a map. It shows the employees where the business should be going, and the employees, through their ideas and efforts, take the business down this path?'

'That's very good,' responded the lady, 'you've got that exactly.'

'So if you needed to change the way you worked then you would need to change the business plan – correct?'

'Precisely . . .'

'I really didn't realise that organizations functioned in this way. I thought that people worked in different departments, and that each department did their own thing, and that it was the manager's job to make it fit the company plan.'

'That was how we used to work before we took a quality approach to the business.'

'A quality approach?'

'Putting the customer's needs first.'

The young student turned a page in his note book and continued writing. The lady picked up her duster and polished the pictures on the wall.

He looked up and cleared his throat softly. 'If people do not work for departments any more, then who do they work for?'

The lady stood for a moment, then went over to the black waste bag in which she had collected all the rubbish. She pulled six crumpled pieces of paper out of the bag and laid them on the small table in front of the young student. 'Let's pretend that each of these crumpled pieces of paper represents a department or function within the Royal Mail. This one could be finance, this one could be facilities, this one engineering – you understand?'

The young man nodded.

'Right – a customer request comes into the organization through this department.' She pointed to one piece of paper. 'That department does the necessary work and then passes the request on to the next department, and so on. Get the idea?'

He nodded but said nothing.

'Each one of these departments is headed by a manager who does a good job. He completes his work within budget and operates his function to meet all the relevant targets. However, meeting departmental targets and budgets does not mean that the customer needs have been met.'

The young man thought about this. 'Does that mean that the departmental targets or budgets were wrong?'

'No. Remember, targets and budgets are forecasts, and a business cannot predict the future, at least not precisely.'

He nodded.

'Let's continue. What would happen if this department further down the chain could not handle the new customer requirement? All the other departments had dealt with their particular process, but this department now had a problem. Say it needed more manpower, more overtime, whatever. What would happen under the department structure?'

The young man raised his hand. 'That manager would fail – or perhaps he might overspend his budgets, or some other customer might suffer just to get this one special customer's order out. That department would have problems.' He pointed to the piece of paper in question.

'Well, yes, I suppose it would – but what is the real problem?'

'The real problem?' He looked thoughtful. 'The manager in that department had not anticipated this customer's possible needs and therefore could be in conflict with his boss?'

She smiled. 'You are right when you mention conflict – *but* what is the real problem?'

He shook his head.

'OK, let's look at it this way. All businesses have processes; unfortunately most do not know what they are. Imagine a pipeline, and that at one end a customer requirement goes in, and at the other end the customer needs come out. Intersecting the pipeline at various points are the processes of the business.'

He nodded in agreement.

'Think about the process of making a cup of tea,' said the lady. 'What's the first process?'

'Well you would get the kettle.'

'No . . .'

'Wait – wait a minute. I know! You'd get the teabags?'

'No . . .'

He bit on his bottom lip. 'You'd turn the tap on?'

'No . . .'

'OK I give up – what is the first process?'

The lady looked at him and smiled. 'The first part of the process is a thirsty customer.'

Looking a little annoyed the young man retaliated. 'Ah, but what about if I make a cup of tea for myself? There is no customer.' He looked smugly at the lady, thinking he had found a flaw in her argument.

'If you make a cup of tea for yourself then you are the customer. You do not make a cup of tea for the sake of making a cup of tea. You see, that's what was wrong with the functional or departmental type of management. Departments did things for the sake of doing them – to justify their existence. Departments lost sight of their real purpose.'

He nodded in acknowledgement of the fact that he had missed the point again. He scribbled down some notes in his book.

The lady picked up her brush and started to sweep the floor. 'You do not come to work to file invoices or to work for the purchasing department – you must be part of a process.'

He took a deep breath, 'But the Royal Mail do not make an end product, so how can you have processes in a pipeline?'

'We have a mails' pipeline,' answered the lady. 'We start with a posting customer and end with a receiving customer. As the mail flows through the pipeline, various processes happen to it, like sorting or segregation. By breaking down the tasks into processes we measure the effectiveness of each process.'

'What's the difference between an effective process and an efficient process?'

The lady smiled. 'That's a very good question. I think I can answer that by saying that a process is efficient if it involves putting right things which have gone wrong. A process is effective if the process is right first time and stays right.'

His head bent over his knees as he continued writing.

'You have still not answered the question I asked five minutes ago – what is the real problem regarding the department style of running a business?'

He shook his head.

She sat down beside him with her brush still in her hand. 'The customer has been let down. It does not matter that three departments were on target and within budget – if one part of the business fails, then the whole business fails. The customer does not see the business as separate departments. The customer perceives the organization as a whole.'

The young student's face was illuminated by knowledge. 'So by using a quality approach to the business, everyone works for the CUSTOMER – now I understand why problem-solving teams are cross-boundary. That way the customer, and not the business, becomes the focus.' He underlined a few words in his notepad. 'To change from the department system to a quality approach style must cost money and upset some people, so what are the benefits?'

The lady walked over to the other side of the room and opened a closet door. She started to take out her coat and put it on. As she buttoned up her coat she said, 'The old way of functional management means people carry out low-skilled repetitive tasks and then hand them over to someone else. It perpetuated the 'bosses and worker style' – us and them. Employees could not make decisions, even though they knew of improvements that could be made to their jobs and to the end product. One job depended on another just like the production line – many employees did not see or understand the finished product. Now, management by process – a quality approach – is the exact opposite. People are multi-skilled and are involved in a variety of tasks sometimes from beginning to end. People constantly receive training. Bosses become coaches and leaders, and the whole process works like one big team. Employees are being empowered and continuous improvement is becoming a way of life.'

'Slow down a bit, I cannot write as fast as you can talk! Does this give you a competitive edge?'

'You are asking some very good questions. Yes, working in a quality way has improved the outcomes – they are faster, more effective, and more consistent. Remember, there is enough competition outside the business: you do not need to create competition within the business.'

'I see . . .' He continued writing. 'How hard was it to get everyone to change – I guess that must have been very difficult?'

She nodded reflectively. 'Yes, change is very difficult for all of us but we could see that if we did not change to meet customer demands then our competition would. I have to admit that change was more difficult for some than others – even now some of our people talk about the good old days.' She walked to the door. 'I have enjoyed our chat, but I have to go now.'

'Oh, before you go, may I ask what your job is?'

She turned and smiled. 'I am surprised you have to ask that question after our talk. Perhaps you have not fully understood?'

He look confused and rather embarrassed. 'Sorry . . . I don't understand.'

'Well ,' she continued, 'what do you think my job is?'

'I . . . er . . . I'm not very good at guessing these things; I'm worried that I may say the wrong thing.'

She laughed softly. 'Well, I do not want to embarrass you, but after our conversation I thought you could have guessed what my job is. Let me tell you.' She turned to open the office door and, looking back over her shoulder she said, 'My job is to get customer letters to their door.'

'But I thought you were . . . well . . . a . . . cleaner?'

She looked at him thoughtfully. 'You have not fully understood the conversation we have just had. I am part of the process, part of the team that makes this business. This office is part of the environment. Other members of the process cannot work in dirty conditions with waste materials lying around. They need a clean and tidy environment in which to do their work – to complete their part of the process, which is delivering a customer's letter to its destination. I perform a cleaning process as part of the mail's pipeline.' With that, she left.

The young student sat quietly for a few moments. He closed his notepad, pushed his pen into his coat pocket and stood up. He looked around the room and walked over to the door. His brain was in overdrive. 'I don't think I need to see the General Manager now, I have no more questions to ask.: When I write my report and tell the lecturer that a clean . . . a member of the Royal Mail gave me all this information, he will think that I have spoken to the Managing Director not the General Manager. I'd like to work here, I can't wait to do my presentation.'

The moral of the story

For an organization to have a total quality approach, then everyone must be adding value to the customer product. Every process should be adding value to the customer product. Every action should be adding value to the customer product.

The organization must focus as one team, with every member just as important as the next. Every member must support and help each other.

Discussion points/questions

1. Would your cleaning staff respond in the same way as the lady in the story? If not, why not?

2. Can you draw your organization's 'pipe line' and identify the processes that feed into it?

3. Does your organization work through a rigid departmental structure, or through a customer'driven structure?

How to delight your customer

This is a true story – a story of the unexpected – a story that could shock you.

One evening I returned home from a business trip at 5:10 p.m. to find that my house had been burgled some time that afternoon. The thief had tried and failed to jemmy open the UPVC backdoor, so he had smashed the small double-glazed window in the door with a brick, and gained entry. Fortunately, my house is alarmed and although the thief gained entry, my alarm activated when he stepped into the sitting-room. Nothing of value was taken, as the alarm obviously frightened the individual, and he left.

The mess and the shock were disturbing. However after ringing the police, I pondered what to do about the broken window in the back door. I needed to get it blocked up and secured overnight so that I could sort out the insurance details the next day. I do not know why – but I rang the organization who had installed the back door. Its name was Anglian Windows.

The time had now just turned 5:30 p.m., the phone rang for some time and I began to think that the people must have gone home for the day. Just as I was about to replace the receiver, a voice answered.

'Anglian Windows, Pat Hacks speaking, how may I help you?'

I explained who I was and what had happened. I mentioned to the young lady on the other end of the phone that Anglian Windows had installed the back door unit some two years previously. 'Is there anything you can do to help me secure my property?' I said.

'Of course there is sir. Leave this with me for ten minutes and I will call you back. I need to ring someone to give you assistance.'

She did not hesitate – Pat Hacks had been empowered to make a decision. She had been empowered to help customers. I was at this moment impressed with the words I heard, but as I put the phone down a doubt came over my mind. 'This is a double glazing company – I bought the door some two years ago – why would they want to help me? – I wonder how much this is going to cost?'

I returned to the chore of trying to pick up the small shattered fragments of glass from my kitchen floor. I could not stop worrying. 'Anglian Windows will not ring back so I had better go and find my home insurance and see if there is an emergency number I can ring – maybe they can help.'

Just then, the phone rang.

'Hello Mr Gatiss, this is Pat Hacks from Anglian Windows. I have contacted Steve Perry from our Liverpool Office and he will be coming to your home within the next hour to secure your back door.'

I was not only impressed but relieved. I could get on with cleaning up the mess and not worry about securing my property overnight.

My wife arrived home just after six and I had to explain the presence of the police car in our drive and the turmoil in the kitchen. I also told her about the Anglian representative coming out within the hour to cover up the hole in the back door.

'I bet that is going to cost something – I hope the insurance company will pay?' I remember her saying. I looked at my watch, it was getting near to 7 p.m.

The phone rang. It was Steve Perry from Anglian Windows ringing on his car phone, to tell me he was stuck in traffic and would be a little late. I told my wife.

When it got to 7:15 p.m. the phone rang again. It was Steve Perry telling me that he was now out of the traffic jam and would be with me shortly.

He arrived at 7:30 p.m. We chatted over a cup of coffee while he boarded up the back door with thick plywood.

'I think I have a centre piece that will fit this door back in Liverpool. It is not the same design, but it will make the door sound until you decide what you are going to do. Would you like me to come back tomorrow and fit it for you?'

I told him I would, but that I would need to check with my insurance company first. I would ring him in the morning.

He had secured my property and left before 8 p.m.

The following day was a Wednesday. I contacted my insurance company. They told me they would need to send an assessor out to my property and that they could not do that until Thursday at the earliest. I would need an original letter-headed quotation which would need to be sent to them. Whatever I did in the mean time was my responsibility.

I rang Pat Hacks at Anglian and explained that I needed a quotation. I asked her to do one immediately for me using the measurements from the records from two years ago, and I asked her to post it First Class that day. I also asked her if Steve Perry could fit the different centre piece to the door, until I sorted out the insurance. My wife and I felt very vulnerable with just a piece of plywood over the door. I then photographed the back door with my video camera, so that the insurance assessor would be able to view the damage when he arrived. I anticipated that Anglian would action my temporary replacement quickly.

The quotation was delivered to my house before 1 p.m. that day by Pat Hacks herself.

Steve Perry rang me and arranged to come out that evening again at 7:30

p.m. to fit the new centre piece to the door. He arrived on time, fitted the new centre piece, and took the old one away all within thirty minutes.

On Thursday the insurance assessor examined the damaged door frame, watched the video that I had taken, and immediately gave me permission to proceed with ordering a new door. However, he said that I would have to pay the £50 excess on my insurance.

Not only had this break-in been upsetting and disrupted work opportunities, but it was now going to cost me £50 as well. I was furious.

I rang Anglian Windows and spoke to Pat Hacks, explaining that I would be placing the order when I received the cheque from the insurance company. I mentioned in conversation that my insurance company insisted on me having to pay £50 towards the cost of the door. Her response was astounding.

'If you place the order with us for your new door and send the cheque with the order, we will give you a £50 discount.'

The order was placed with the cheque – the new door and frame were fitted.

I wrote to the Managing Director of Anglian Windows, Mr Ron Swift, to congratulate him on *delighting* a customer. His response was short and modest.

' It is always good to receive such letters as yours. Unfortunately people will write quite readily with bad news but not too often with good. Anglian as a company are always striving to provide a quality service to our customers. We do not always succeed, but we try very hard.'

The moral of the story
A customer is for life not just the guarantee period.

Discussion points/questions

1. Are your staff, who are at the point of contact with the customer, empowered to respond immediately to all customer problems? If not, should they be?

2. Does your product carry a lifetime support guarantee? If not, why not?

Quality for hire

A newly married couple were in the process of moving into a new flat which they had decided to rent in an upmarket part of town.

On the morning of their move, they were busily unloading their possessions when they noticed an expensive-looking widescreen television and a very modern video recorder on the carpet, under a desk.

'I didn't realize that the flat came with extras as impressive as this!' exclaimed Steve, who was mesmerized by the technology before his eyes.

'Hang on a moment, here's a note which must be from the previous tenants,' said his wife, Sarah. 'It says that the rental firm will stop by some time on Tuesday to pick up the TV and the video.'

'Oh well,' sighed Steve. 'I thought it was too good to be true.'

They continued to unpack their belongings.

Three days later, on the Tuesday, Sarah made a point of staying in the whole time, so that she wouldn't miss the person who was coming to collect the TV and video. By the end of the afternoon, however, there had been no sign of the hire company, and no phone call from them to explain the delay. Sarah was understandably annoyed and when her husband returned from work, she told him of her frustration.

'It's not that I needed to go out for any reason, it just would have been nice to know that I could have done.' Steve was sympathetic, and suggested that his wife call up the nearest branch of the hire company the next day, to request an explanation.

The following morning, Sarah called up the company and told them about the note that the previous tenants had left, giving the address. The young man on the other end of the phone had a slightly nervous tone in his voice as he informed Sarah that he had no record of a television or video ever having been rented out to that address. Sarah was so surprised by this information that she didn't know what to say next, and she just put the phone down.

Speaking with her husband that evening, Sarah momentarily suggested that they should keep the TV and video, but Steve didn't think it was a good idea.

'I'd feel guilty because it isn't ours, and I'd worry about the hire company blaming us when they eventually find out they've made a mistake.'

It was decided that Sarah should call up again the next day, and demand to speak to the manager.

When she got through to the manager the next morning, Sarah was in determined mood.

'The previous tenant wouldn't have left that note for no reason: I really think you should double-check your records and get to the bottom of this, because I wasted a whole day on Tuesday sitting in, when I could have been out buying things we need for our new flat.'

'Of course, madam, I shall take whatever action is necessary to find out the truth in this situation. Thank you so much for calling me. I shall get back to you as soon as I have any news.'

After holding private discussions with each of his employees that day, the manager was able to discover what had happened.

When the previous tenants of the flat had called late on Friday to announce that they were moving and so terminating their hire contract, the employee who took the call told them correctly, that the TV and video would be collected on the following Tuesday. However, when he put the phone down and jotted the information on to the relevant form, he realized that he was supposed to be meeting friends in a pub, and that he was going to be a couple of minutes late. Instead of making sure that the document was passed to the van driver's department, he put it to one side of his desk, and left.

Returning to work on the Monday, the employee accidentally placed a file on top of the document and didn't discover it again until the next morning, by which time he knew it would be too late to incorporate the pick-up into the driver's timetable. He threw the document in the bin, desperately hoping that the problem would just disappear.

When Sarah had phoned on the Wednesday, the same employee had taken the call and had told her – in an attempt to cover his tracks – that he had no record of such an address.

Although the manager of the branch felt compelled to warn the employee about such foolish behaviour, he decided not to punish him too heavily, as that would have affected staff morale. Instead, he saw it as an opportunity to enhance the quality approach which the senior management were in the process of introducing.

In consultation with all his employees, he organized a new system of routing incoming calls directly to the relevant sector. (The original phone call, for example, would now be put straight through to the drivers' department which, as a result, feels more involved in the company's objective, and more valued.) At the monthly meeting, the manager told his colleagues from around the country of his innovation, and it was decided to implement the scheme nationwide.

He called Sarah and Steve to tell them of the results of his inquiry. He thanked them warmly for their help and honesty, and offered to let them rent the TV and video free of charge for a year. Sarah and Steve are now loyal customers of the company.

The moral of the story
It is essential to view the customer in a positive light.
All feedback can be helpful if it is acted upon immediately and correctly.
Customers treated with respect are likely to respond with loyalty.

Discussion points/questions

1. How would your own organization treat an employee such as the one in the story?

2. Was it enough for the branch manager to consult his employees before initiating a new system, or should he have involved them more? If so, how?

3. Try to make a list of all the customers (internal and external) in the story.

4. Put yourself in the position of the Chairman of the hire company. What are the five most important objectives that you would wish to communicate to all your staff throughout the country?

Quality in action

'I am four weeks in arrears,' exclaimed Peter.

'Four weeks, that's a lot of material,' expressed the consultant.

Peter Dunn was the supervisor in the goods inwards department of an international electronics company. It was taking up to four weeks to receive material, count it, inspect it then move it through into the stores for location or issuing to the assembly shops. This delay was causing serious problems creating shortages and line stoppages. The labour budget in the goods inwards department was overspent, as they worked overtime every weekend. It also had major consequences for the accounts department, who could not pay invoices until they had received confirmation, through a goods inward note (GRN), that material had been received. This led to many suppliers ringing up, chasing payment, and often refusing to supply more materials until accounts had been settled. Customer orders were also being delayed, and this was reflected in lower turnover figures.

Overall the situation was unacceptable, so the Managing Director called in a consultant to assess and advise on the situation.

The consultant looked at Peter and smiled. 'Over the last three days, I have been watching what your department does, and I would just like to check that my understanding is correct. Could I explain to you, what I think your operation is doing?'

'Certainly,' responded Peter.

The consultant read from his notes. 'Material is ordered by the purchasing department using the computer system. You get a hard copy of the purchase order, which you file in supplier sequence. When material arrives from the supplier, your department unload and place the goods on a waiting shelf. Each shelf is numbered and dated, and the day log book is cross-referenced with this information.' He looked at Peter for confirmation.

Peter nodded, but said nothing.

'You have people allocated to do specific duties. You have someone unloading transport and placing material on to the waiting shelf. You have other people picking material off the shelf, in date order, checking the supplier details and then counting the material. You then book the material in, on a computer generated goods receiving note. One of your staff then files your copy of the GRN with the supplier order, and a copy of the GRN is sent to the accounts department.' Again he looked at Peter for confirmation.

'Yes, that's right.'

'Your staff then move the material from the goods inwards area into the stores, where someone locates the material for future use, or it is issued to the assembly line.'

'Exactly right.' Peter sat back heavily in his chair while his extended hand tapped nervously on the desk.

The consultant stopped reading from his notes and looked at Peter. 'So, what do you think is the problem?'

'That's easy,' said Peter. 'The problem is I have not got enough people to do the job.'

It was later that afternoon when the consultant found himself sitting in front of the Managing Director summarizing his findings.

'In brief I have identified a number of problem areas which need addressing. There are short-term, and long-term problems. The short-term problems are based around internal customer problems. The long-term problems are based around external customer problems.'

'What do you suggest?'

'I suggest we set up a task force team which will consist of personnel from the goods inwards, purchasing, accounts, the shop floor and the computer departments. Under my facilitation, this team will use the PANDA Problem Solving Discipline technique, and by utilizing some quality tools, we will structure a recovery programme.'

'How long will that take?'

'It will take a few days to set up the meeting with all the participants. It will then take around three meetings to establish some plan of action. It depends on the plan of action, but I would anticipate that you will see some significant positive results within twelve weeks.'

'OK, let's do it.'

The first meeting of the task force team was scheduled to last from ten o'clock in the morning until three o'clock on the afternoon. Sandwiches were supplied so the team did not have to disperse for lunch. This first meeting was taken up with heated discussion on proposing what the problem was. It ended with everyone agreeing that the problem was:

'The material input system is adversely affecting customer satisfaction.'

Because the definition identified that the customer was affected, it made the problem a company problem – a problem for everyone, not just the goods inwards people.

The second meeting was scheduled for an afternoon and overran into the evening. The reason for the extended meeting was due to the teams' enthusiasm and involvement, as the consultant introduced them to Team Affinity Brainstorming.

At the third meeting the consultant had prepared the cause and effect diagram and the team were keen to learn the techniques of the critical success factor matrix. From this information they allocated resources and set up projects. Using many quality tools and techniques they measured and controlled activities resulting in many significant changes that resulted in elimination or reduction of waste.

It was the members of the team who persuaded their colleagues to change working practices. The management took no part in this process. The management gave visible support through an active open programme of recognition and reward. They did this by regularly walking around the stores and goods receiving areas, and by acknowledging the efforts being made: through newsletters, briefing groups and even bringing customers into the area, which indicated how proud and important the senior managers thought the improvement programme was. The problem was owned by the stakeholders and they took responsibility for their actions.

Results after twelve weeks
- Purchasing persuaded many suppliers to repackage materials and supply certificates of conformance so that material did not have to be counted or inspected. This saved over 50 per cent of the time to book in material.
- Copies of purchase orders were no longer required by the goods inwards department as the computer system was modified to show all necessary details. This alleviated the need for someone to spend over ten hours per week filing and checking orders.
- Goods inwards and stores personnel merged and therefore when material was passed to the stores area for locating or issuing, it was done by the goods receiving person. This ensured that there was less of a delay between moving material. It also ensured that the first person to handle the material, coming in to the organization, took responsibility for the material right up to the point of locating it in the stores. Material no longer went missing. The problems with the old culture of blaming someone else for not doing something disappeared. Stores' personnel were trained to have skills in goods inwards and vice versa.
- Goods received notes were no longer produced by the system. The computer system was modified so that the accounts department could automatically check to see if material from a suppliers' order had been received. This computer check simplified invoice clearance and alleviated work in the accounts department, creating significant labour savings. This also saved filing GRNs both in the goods receiving and the accounts departments.

- Material was booked in within twenty-four hours of being received into the company. This action eliminated overtime. Over 90 per cent of the material shortage problem disappeared, resulting in more effective material planning and finished product programming.
- After six months of operating these new procedures a 20 per cent labour saving was made in the stores and goods receiving department by transferring some of the labour into other departments. This was seen as a positive move as it gave rise for advancement, promotion and new learning opportunities.
- During the following twelve months there was a 20 per cent reduction overall in the company's labour force due to early retirements and natural wastage (people leaving). Many retirees and leavers were not replaced, and all vacancies were taken up with internal transfers. Over 50 per cent of these came from the stores and goods receiving area. Investment, in training and education, will always be more cost-effective than ignorance.

The moral of this story
The solution to many problems generally only comes through a structured, consistent quality approach with stakeholder involvement known as **POW**: participation, ownership and warranty.

Discussion points/questions

1. Would the company have been as successful without the help of the consultant?

2. How important do you think the use of quality tools and techniques were in implementing the changes?

3. What part did the senior management play in implementing the changes?

4. Are copies of the same document filed by more than one department in your organization? How can you reduce the paper-flow? Can you amalgamate jobs or merge functions, to reduce waste?

Quality in the bag

A friend of mine went to a small but very special shop to buy a handbag. She was a loyal customer, and always bought her bags there. She never really thought about the service offered by the shop; it was more of a habit for her to go there.

As usual she was delighted with her purchase, and she used it religiously for the next few weeks. After a couple of months, however, the condition of the bag began to deteriorate rapidly. The material, which was an animal print, became strangely worn so that the bag actually moulted like a real animal.

This posed something of a problem for my friend, who was uncertain as to what to do about it. She felt slight feelings of guilt, as the bag was obviously intended for special occasions, and yet she had used it every day – perhaps, she thought, it was her fault that the bag was falling apart in this way.

After some reflection, she decided that she ought to take the bag back to the store, to see if there was any way in which she could be helped. The store was very low-key in the way that it promoted itself: its prime selling point was its insistence on top quality products, and it was for this reason that my friend opted to test the shop's reaction to her dilemma.

Upon showing the bag to the young sales consultant, and explaining her feelings of guilt over having used the bag too frequently, my friend was taken aback by the intense disappointment that she appeared to have caused. The sales consultant was genuinely horrified that such a thing could have happened to one of her products. My friend had never heard an assistant speak with such pride and responsibility: it was as if she herself had made the bag! She declared that the bag must have been made with a faulty animal skin.

I do not know if faulty products are such a rarity at this shop, but the sales consultant certainly acted as though it was the very first time such a disaster had happened. The effect of this was to make my friend feel very special and highly valued. The young girl called the owner of the shop, who immediately drove over from her home, two miles away, along with her husband. When the owner arrived and saw the bag for herself, she was equally appalled and apologetic.

The owner of the shop took action immediately. She telephoned the factory in a small town near Milan where the bags were made and, in fluent Italian, requested that a new skin should be found as swiftly as possible so that work could begin on a new bag without delay.

After all this commotion, the owner and her husband took my friend into a small room at the back of the shop, made her a cup of coffee, and continued to reassure her that such faulty goods were totally unacceptable, especially with the ultra-competitive nature of the modern marketplace. My friend once again suggested that she had used the bag too much, to which the owner replied, 'The bags are built to last. I have one which I had made for me just after we were married, eleven years ago, and it still looks as good as it did that day. Even if you are producing goods which will only be used once or twice a year, it is essential that they are able to last a lifetime. It is only through a commitment to quality that this shop can survive – we spend very little on advertising because we believe that a satisfied customer is the best form of publicity there is. Customers need quality goods and services, and that is what we must strive to provide.'

This speech was delivered in such a relaxed, low-key manner that my friend did not realize until she got home an hour later that the shop owner had been using language which she usually associated with high-powered businessmen. It was a revelation to hear such a philosophy being expounded by a softly-spoken woman.

My friend has now struck up an acquaintance with the owner of the shop, and she has been introduced to many of her family. She has discovered that every member of the family is involved in the business in some capacity, and that they are all totally committed to a quality approach. Those members of staff who are not part of the family are made to feel as if they really are: the whole operation is such a tight unit that the regular customers (including my friend) are fully aware of the aims and beliefs of the business, and they all feel free to contribute their own ideas.

The moral of this story
When the customer feels a part of the business, she is unlikely to go elsewhere.
The most effective form of marketing is through a delighted customer.
When given feedback from a customer try, whenever possible, to take action there and then.

Discussion points/questions

1. Are there any specific problems which might be encountered by a family business?

2. If a customer complains about a faulty product, and you know that it is a very common complaint, should you tell the customer the truth (admitting your failings), or should you lead the customer to believe that it is a

fault which has never occurred before? Explain the reasoning behind your answer.

3. Is it right for the customer to be aware of the aims and beliefs of an organization, or is it none of her business as long as the products are of quality? Again, explain the reasons for your answer.

4. Imagine you are the woman in the story. After using your replacement bag for a few weeks, the same problem reoccurs. You are now good friends with the shop owner and her family: it will cause embarrassment if you complain again. What do you do?

**Start immediately with the positive thought
that everything you do from now on,
is going to stand for quality . . .**

**. . . everything you do and say is judged by others,
and is stamped with your vision of quality . . .**

. . . make that a vision of excellence.

Suggested Further Reading

Bach, Richard (1973), *Jonathan Livingston Seagull – A Story*: London, Pan Books. This book is about individuals having a mission, and striving to be the best. It is a powerful holistic story of attitude, perseverance and determination: all the attributes for a quality approach.

Bank, John (1992), *The Essence of Total Quality Management*: Hemel Hempstead, Prentice Hall. Looks at the differences between TQM and traditional quality control.

Dale, Barrie G. (1994), *Managing Quality*: Hemel Hempstead, Prentice Hall. This book covers the subject of total quality through extensive case studies. It has many knowledgeable contributors and is a good reference source.

Davidow, W. H. with Uttal, B. (1989), *Total Customer Service*: New York, Harper and Row. The title is fairly self-explanatory: a good guide to the essentials of customer care.

Davis, Stanley with Goetsch, David (1994), *Introduction to Total Quality*: New York, Prentice Hall Macmillan. Looks at the history and development of quality management in the USA, and analyzes the writings of authors such as Deming, Crosby and Juran.

De Bono, E. (1990), *I Am Right You Are Wrong*: London, Penguin Group. This book challenges thinking paradigms and stimulates new ways of looking at our problems and prejudices.

De Bono, E. (1990), *Sur-Petition – Going Beyond Competition*: London, Harper Collins. This book challenges the rules of traditional competition and stimulates new quality strategic thinking for the future.

De Porter, Bobbi (1992), *Quantum Learning – Unleash the Genius Within You*: London, Judy Piatkus. This book introduces new ways of learning that will provide help and guidance for the challenges involved in adopting a quality approach to work and play.

Deming, W. E. (1982), *Quality, Productivity and Competitive Position*: Massachusetts: MIT Centre for Advanced Engineering Study. A detailed book on the philosophies and thoughts of one of the world's top quality gurus.

Deming, W. E. (1986), *Out of Crisis*: Cambridge, Cambridge University Press. The author discusses and expands on the need to be customer focused and to regard the consumer as 'the most important part of the production line'.

Drucker, P. F. (1974), *Management – Tasks, Responsibilities and Practices*: London, Heinemann. This is an encyclopedia of a work, and emphasises Druckers' philosophy of setting objectives. It is a comprehensive management book, packed with case studies.

Drucker, P. F. (1989), *Managing for Results*: London, Heinemann. A book full of case studies and well supported material, showing examples of companies that approach their business in an analytical way.

Goldratt, Eliyahu M. and Cox, Jeff (1989), *The Goal*: Hants, England: Gower Publishing. The book is written as a love story – but it has some very powerful and revealing solutions to some organizational problems.

Handy, C. (1976), *Understanding Organisations*: London, Penguin Books. A comprehensive analysis of how organizations work. The book is packed with case studies and sound management practices.

Handy, C. (1986), *The Future of Work*: Oxford, Basil Blackwell. The author proposes that lifetime careers are becoming a thing of the past, and that to survive in the future people will need to have a range of jobs. The book emphasises that a quality approach to this changing paradigm is necessary.

Imai, Masaaki (1986), *Kaizen – The Key to Japan's Competitive Success*: London, McGraw Hill. Kaizen means gradual, unending improvement, doing things, 'little things', better. It is the Japanese philosophy of quality. The book is full of examples and is a thought-provoking text.

Olsen, Michael with Teare, Richard and Gummesson, Evert (1996), *Service Quality in Hospitality Organizations*: London, Cassell. Explains the importance of quality to all those working in the hospitality industry, including a good range of case studies.

Peter, Laurence F. and Hull, Raymond (1994), *The Peter Principle*: London, Souvenir Press. This book is a humorous look at why things go wrong. Its strength lies in the fact that many of the examples are very true to life and support the need for a quality approach.

Peters, T. (1988), *Thriving on Chaos*: London, Macmillan. A detailed comprehensive work on planning and managing change and why adopting a quality approach is essential.

Peters, T. and Austin, Nancy (1990), *A Passion for Excellence – The Leadership Difference*: Glasgow, William Collins Sons & Co. The title of the book says it all. It is full of common sense and emphasises superior customer service, constant innovation, and using the abilities of every employee within the company.

Peters, T. and Waterman, R. H. Jr (1982), *In Search of Excellence*: New York & London, Harper and Row. The book analyzes many USA organizations through case studies. It identifies and benchmarks the good and bad practices. Although the work was carried out in the early 1980s, this book has many relevant points to make about adopting a quality approach in today's environment.

Teare, Richard with Atkinson, Cyril and Westwood, Clive (1993), *Achieving Quality Performance*: London, Cassell. Provides detailed examples of six award-winning quality improvement programmes, implemented by companies including Land Rover and ICL.